# A Five Year Plan for Geraniums

# A Five Year Plan for Geraniums

*Growing Flowers Commercially in East Germany 1946–1989*

Judith M. Taylor

**To order additional copies of this book, contact:**
Xlibris
1-888-795-4274
www.Xlibris.com
Orders@Xlibris.com
790038

Table of contents

IN MEMORY OF BLANCHE AND ELI

No matter how you shuffled the kaleidoscope of Germany's map, the significance of Erfurt and Quedlinburg for floriculture remained paramount. These were the powerhouses of German horticulture from long before the First World War and remained central to its dominance in the eastern bloc until the fall of the Berlin Wall and reunification.

POST-WORLD WAR ONE (1918)
North Sea
SWEDEN
DENMARK
Baltic Sea
EAST PRUSSIA (GERM.)
NETH.
Elbe R.
Weser R.
Oder R.
Berlin
POLAND
Harz Mtns
Quedlinburg
BELG.
Dresden
Erfurt
LUX.
GERMANY
CZECHOSLOVAKIA
FRANCE
AUSTRIA
HUNGARY
SWITZERLAND
ROM.
ITALY
YUGOSLAVIA
0 100 200km
0 100 200mi

## The contribution of Klaus Hoffmann

Klaus Hoffmann's work is key to mine. Based on some findings in the research for two previous books, *Visions of Loveliness: Great Flower Breeders of the Past* and *An Abundance of Flowers: More Great Flower Breeders of the Past*, in which several significant figures lived and worked behind the Iron Curtain, I decided to pursue the story of what happened to German floriculture during the period of Socialism, 1946 to 1989.

Klaus Hoffmann (b. 1938) is an experienced horticulturist and author of a history of East German floriculture. In 2015, he published "Der Zierplflanzenbau in Mitteldeuschtland des 19. und 20. Jahrhunderts - Bertrachtungen über 200 Jahre Produktion und Zücthtung." ("Flower nurseries in Middle Germany in the 19th and 20th centuries- more than two hundred years of flower breeding and production.") (Notschriften Verlag Radebeul). (ref--) He worked in nurseries both under Socialism and in the aftermath of 1989. Nothing replaces the experience of being there at the time.

By a very happy turn of fate, I was able to get a copy of this book. It provided me with an enormous amount of information which would otherwise have been very hard to find, and Klaus Hoffman has very graciously allowed me to make whatever use of it I wish. Hoffmann's book forms the basis of the work which follows. The great value of his book is its clear documentation of chapter and verse. Facts are king.

The way I learned about the book was because over the years I have had the great privilege and good fortune to be in touch with Andrea Ludwig, the daughter of one of the best-known horticulturists in Dresden, Wilhelm Elsner (1921 – 2013). Frau Ludwig ran the business until a few years ago. She has since handed it on to her niece, Antonia Feindura. Frau Feindura's husband Martin is the chief executive officer of the firm.

Wilhelm Elsner, the grandson of the founder, specialized in pelargoniums—or geraniums, as they are more widely known to the public. The firm, which is now known as PAC Elsner, was started by Wilhelm's grandfather in 1889 and continued under the ownership of his father. Wilhelm III then inherited the business from his own father. The term "PAC" is derived from the first initials of the principal flowers they grew: pelargonium, anthurium, and chrysanthemum. As the Elsners became known for their pelargoniums throughout the world, Wilhelm Elsner II decided to focus almost solely on this plant and in 1926 issued his first catalogue.

His son Wilhelm was also passionate about these flowers, and constantly looked for new and better forms by breeding his own cultivars. He introduced cultivars which were resistant to disease and very long-blooming. Even during the Socialist period, 1946 to 1989, some brave enthusiasts in the United States and the United Kingdom, such as David Lemon in Lompoc, managed to get hold of his plants and promote them in the west.

Throughout the latter part of this tempestuous period, Klaus Hoffmann, who had studied horticulture at the Humboldt University in Berlin, started working for Elsner as his manager in 1989 and stayed until he retired in 2003. Hoffmann had also worked in nurseries in other parts of East Germany, particularly in Erfurt and Quedlinburg. As a native of East Germany during his formative years, he knew the scene and how to manage.

Herr Hoffmann also examined the history of some other companies affected by the political conditions who were in the same plight. His book was translated for me by Leslie Harlson and Clare Drews between 2014 and 2017. Wilhelm Elsner himself published his own memoirs in 2005, "Lebenserinnerungen." (ref—)

For readers who would like to learn more about this topic pleases see the list of books at the end.

## Introduction

"Consider the lilies of the field, they toil not, neither do they spin." So pretty, so gentle, so apolitical—but in post-World War Two Europe, so wrong.

The dubious experiment in political economy and social engineering known as Socialism, which distorted the functioning of Russia and the Eastern European countries and did horrifying damage to their populations for much of the twentieth century, left its mark on many industries. One industry which has not received as much attention as other, larger ones, is horticulture, with its subsector of floriculture.

This introduction gives a brief overview of what happened to floriculture in East Germany between 1946 and 1989. Several key factors strike one at the outset. Before World War Two, 1939 to 1945, Germany had been a leading contender in the European floriculture trade. This is not widely known, as the Netherlands take up all the oxygen. Three cities in the eastern provinces of Thuringia and Saxony provided the bulk of the seed, plants, and cut flowers for that trade: Erfurt, Quedlinburg, and Dresden, with their surrounding smaller communities. Berlin also had several notable seed and plant companies.

It was a political and historical fluke that these cities were part of East Germany after the country was divided in late 1945, but their presence led to East Germany dominating that sector of Europe. This was so even after the socialist government had done its best to wreck everything. Floriculture was not as modernized and developed in the other Eastern European countries as in East Germany, though Czechoslovakia, Poland, and Hungary came the closest.

At the end of World War II, Germany was occupied by the United States, Great Britain, France, and the Soviet Union. This partition was necessary to make sure that the country could never regain its dominant status and threaten the stability of the rest of the world. In the vacuum created by the war, the Soviet Union also managed to take over several smaller Eastern European countries by one means or another.

On October 7, 1949, after the period of *de facto* division between the four powers, the former Soviet sector of Germany formally became the Deutsche Demokratische Republik, usually referred to as "East Germany" or in German the "DDR." This split the largest country in Europe into two separate nations. The separation lasted for about 40 years, more than one generation.

The East German Communist party took charge but the offshoots were called Socialist, not Communist.

When eventually the two countries were reunited in 1989, the younger generation in East Germany was vastly different from the same cohort in West Germany. Getting them to merge and blend into one nation was a far more difficult and costly undertaking than had been anticipated. The previous chancellor of Germany, Angela Merkel, grew up in the DDR.

Within a few years after the end of the war, there were sufficient countries under the aegis of the Soviet Union to comprise a separate hostile bloc within Europe, COMECON. These are the initials of the English translation for the economic bloc across Eastern Europe. Partly because of its sheer size and the fact that Germany had always been a very efficient society, East Germany was the leading nation within that bloc. The fact that the Soviet Union had to maintain virtual garrisons in all these countries indicates that the terms by which they governed were not by popular consent in most cases.

In the case of floriculture, there were some special circumstances favoring the DDR. Before World War Two, Germany had a very effective and thriving floricultural industry. World-famous rosarians and other great flower breeders flourished primarily in the Eastern provinces of Saxony, Thuringia, and

Saxony-Anhalt. The engines of this flourishing trade were the cities of Erfurt and Quedlinburg, plus Berlin and Dresden. A combination of natural geographical and climatic factors propelled the development of horticulture in those cities forward from mediaeval times. Once Germany had been divided, East Germany had the advantage of keeping these flower-growing cities. Other smaller, satellite towns and villages also involved in floriculture surrounded them.

The economies of the Eastern countries, including the Soviet Union itself, were under the control of the governments and their policies. Ultimate control rested in Moscow. The Soviet government laid down the terms which governed economic activity in Eastern Europe. These policies were followed with varying degrees of ruthlessness in the different countries but violence—even terror, force, and confiscation—were the principal methods of enforcement.

When things went wrong, as they inevitably did, the central authorities were not interested in finding the reason for the failure, but only looked for culprits to blame and shift responsibility. Because of this lack of insight, the same mistakes were made over and over again. Anyone who dared to disagree was rapidly silenced.

## Brief history of the USSR

The author begs the reader's indulgence for a rapid overview of how the Soviet Union slashed its path, providing a setting for what is to follow before she returns to the straight and narrow of the theme.

Historically, extreme endemic inequality has led to great cycles of revolution and counter-revolution. It was no different in Russia. In Tsarist times, greater Russia had been very backward. The pioneering efforts of Peter the Great to catch up with the West had faded. The country remained essentially an agrarian society and there was very little lucrative industry of any sort. The nobility who owned the land were rich, supported by timber and crops from their land. There was hardly any middle class. Peasants were tied to the land as serfs and had nothing. Even after ceasing to be serfs, they still had almost no disposable income or political power.

There was no incentive for improvement until the balance of power could be shifted. By the mid-nineteenth century, intellectuals saw the problem and became restless. They wrote books, they talked endlessly, and a few turned to anarchy in despair. In 1881 one of them assassinated Tsar Alexander II. It led nowhere except for the rebels who died or were executed.

The assassination was a real pity but resulted from the radical view that a moderate leader was more dangerous than an outright dictator. The public would cherish the moderate and he would thus stand in the way of fundamental change. This tsar had liberated the serfs and had made a number of other useful reforms. It was Tsar Alexander who sold Alaska to the United States in 1867. That was very useful to the United States.

After the 1917 Bolshevik revolution in Russia, Vladimir Lenin, and later Joseph Stalin, the new leaders, decided that their most important goal was to industrialize as fast as they could. They wanted to become equal with or even surpass the rest of the world. A massive redistribution of wealth could erase the glaring inequalities that had held the country back for so long. A source of capital for construction and machinery was needed quickly. Alas, this was the ultimate oxymoron. No sensible nation would give the Bolsheviks a line of credit, and even Armand Hammer, the left-leaning American millionaire, could not do it by himself.

The solution was to use the agricultural sector as the source of money to build an industrial society, financing from within. They based this program on the lands they had seized from the nobility. Sales of crops and timber could bring money and thus capital, allowing the government to begin industrialization. Everything was to be planned centrally, using five years as a unit of accomplishment. Provincial leaders received instructions, but were not allowed to question anything or make any objections. All they had to do was to meet the targets set for them within five years.

Organizing the townspeople—the "proletariat"—into factory workers was not too difficult, but dealing with the unruly, scattered, and obstinate farmworkers to wring out enough money for state projects was another matter. Lenin's delight in the rule of the proletariat did not extend to peasants. In many ways, these characteristics made Russia the worst possible country in which to create a socialist state.

The market had to be centralized and controlled by the state in such a way that no individual could benefit from the work involved in growing the crops. The producers were to receive merely a subsistence level of reward. This system marked a return to medieval peonage. As is always the case with scoundrels, the leaders made a call for patriotism as its own reward.

The watchword was collectivization followed by centralized planning. The peasantry first had to be collectivized, i.e., farms and agricultural businesses had to be removed from private ownership and turned over to the state. The highly successful local farmers, the so-called "kulaks," who did a much better job than the others in their villages and had become fairly rich, particularly irked the Party. Getting rid of them was a priority.

Once collectivized, the farming sector was subjected to centralized planning aimed at various theoretical targets which may or may not have borne any relation to reality. There were at least two Five-Year Plans for East Germany as a whole. The second one was not too successful, so it was changed into a Seven-Year Plan. This approach was known as a "command economy." The ultimate laudable intention was that full industrialization would lift everyone's income and diminish the blatant inequality resulting from former policies. This policy did offer some relief to chronically deprived segments of the population but at a rather steep price of loss of autonomy. How far it missed the mark is now a matter of historical record.

After the Second World War, Russia seized control of much of Eastern Europe and began putting versions of this same system into effect in those countries. This was assisted by the interpersonal dynamics at the Yalta Conference in 1944. The purpose of the conference was to sort out the future of Europe once the war was over but Franklin Roosevelt was already very frail by 1944. In his weakened state, Roosevelt was no match for Stalin, and instead sided with him against Churchill because of Roosevelt's lifelong distrust of the British and their hopes for retaining their empire. Churchill saw what was happening but no longer had any leverage. These seemingly minor aspects of very serious events led to Russia being rewarded for its aggression.

No industry was exempt, but little or nothing has been written in English about the effects of this process on horticulture and floriculture in East Germany during the post-Second World War decades until the collapse of the Soviet Union and freeing of the satellite republics in 1989. Well-run nursery businesses were seized peremptorily without compensation. Some of the workers were enrolled in collectives. The owners had to leave with nothing but their personal effects. If they stayed, they were subject to ruinous rules. This all happened while the population was still reeling from the loss of the war and utter destruction of their country.

State-run organizations of varying quality and competence replaced the previous system, starting a few years after the end of the war and continuing to take over and modify the nurseries until the 1970s. When Russia (formerly the USSR) and Eastern Europe collapsed in 1989, no one was prepared for the free-for-all that followed. The lumbering socialist system ceased to be relevant, but very few individuals were nimble enough to deal with a capitalist world. Suddenly it became difficult to make a living in floriculture. Years in a collective left many unable to fend for themselves. Only the small businesses which had been operating under the radar were able to continue more or less the way they had been doing before.

The title of this book is intentionally tongue-in-cheek. There may not actually have been a five-year plan for geraniums, but once the floricultural industry was firmly under the thumb of the socialist government in East Germany, the new leaders treated it like any other industry. They chose mostly well-qualified people to be in charge of the collectives and then imposed their authority over them. The local and regional leaders thought they could make decisions about what should be grown, how much of it and where it was to be sold—in other words, plans. Regardless of that, anything they did was open to being second-guessed by remote authorities in the USSR.

Planning is not necessarily a dirty word. Without it, no business could grow and succeed. Before the socialist takeover, the prominent large nurseries carefully chose what they would grow, based on what they knew would sell—otherwise known as planning. They also knew they needed almost constant innovation to stay ahead of their competitors. It is when the plans are made without regard to local conditions and business realities that they go badly astray. Moscow's reach was very long.

In almost all businesses, "new and improved" versions of the product are essential to company growth. It is a perennial marketing strategy. In floriculture, experts constantly crossed promising plants, seeking longer-blossoming, larger flowers, new colors, disease resistance, and other very desirable traits.

According to classical economic theory, the public benefited from the array of choices because it led to competition over price.

Redundancy and overlap were part of the process, a sort of creative turmoil, even disruption. There could be a glut of frilly pink gladioli one year and double mauve petunias another. This is an inherently untidy process. Socialist leaders, on the other hand, did not like untidiness. Everything had to have a place and be accounted for. Procrustes' bed comes to mind. Logical? Well, yes and no. Read on and we shall see.

As one reads through Hoffmann's descriptions of early nurseries, his narrative is inextricably wound up with the fates they suffered after World War Two. He organized his work geographically, covering each business as a whole, pre- and post-socialism.

Here is a brief lexicon of a few of the terms Hoffmann used to describe the situation in the DDR under Socialism. The meaning of some others will become clear in context.

DSG: Deutsche Saatgut Gesellschaft. German Seed Association

GPG: Gärtnerischen Produktionsgenossenschafte. Horticultural Cooperative

LPG: Landwirtschaftliche Produktionsgenossenschafte. Agricultural Cooperative

VEB: Volkseigenes Betrieb. "People–owned" enterprise. The "people" means the state, i.e. the government, owned it

VEG: Volkseigenes Gut. People–owned farm. A VEG could be part of a central or regional group of similar businesses, sometimes connected with a university.

ZfS: Central Office for Variety Registration

Winston Churchill's metaphor of an Iron Curtain applied very aptly to the inhabitants of the DDR. They were sealed off from all contact with the rest of the world. Added to all their difficulties, making a living became particularly uncertain. The initial model for the new country was communist society in the Soviet Union, administered by the military and only slightly adapted to local conditions. It is hard to overestimate the effect of such sweeping changes on a people already reeling from wartime devastation before they even had time to take stock of what had happened to them.

Rules and regulations created by the Soviet Union in the 1920s to be applied in satellite countries and help them to adapt to Leninist-Stalinist ideas were very hard to understand. The laws were in direct contradiction to constitutional principles and were applied quite arbitrarily. It is true that really democratic and constitutional principles had been lacking in Germany for many years before, but the population not unreasonably expected some semblance of them in a new postwar world.

There are two main reasons this book will deal largely with East Germany, the DDR. One is the existence of Klaus Hoffmann's book and the information it contains. The other is that even a segment of Germany, East Germany, was still a formidable country in its own right and dominated the rest of Eastern Europe. A further factor is the German tradition of keeping very good records. That did not extend to some of the other COMECON countries, the economic bloc comprising Eastern Europe under Soviet domination.

The level of deprivation in post war Germany was staggering. Many millions of men and a lot of women had been killed. Food was nonexistent. There was almost no habitable space, no fuel, and no transport. Everything was in ruins. Few people in other countries were able to feel very sorry for the Germans, but the lessons of the First World War had been learned the hard way. It was essential to reverse this decline fast. In West Germany, the Marshall Plan began to improve conditions for the public with great success, but General Marshall and President Truman were not about to help a Communist country.

There are anecdotes about Germans who had been interned in England as enemy aliens returning to Germany in the fall of 1945 being utterly confused and dazed as they sought their old homes in the rubble-strewn, flattened cities. "Here you are. This is it. Cheerio," said the English soldiers who had escorted them back.

## Chapter 1: Horticulture and floriculture in Germany

Horticulture is a specialized branch of agriculture. The word horticulture stems from the Latin word for a garden, "hortus." The main difference lies in the scale of the endeavor. Agriculture deals with very large fields, usually planted with a single crop. Horticulture deals with smaller plots of land, such as an enclosed garden or an orchard, and encompasses many types of crop at once. Much of horticulture applies to edible crops but one branch is limited to crops grown solely for their appearance and fragrance: ornamental horticulture or floriculture.

Ornamental horticulture and floriculture involve the supply of trees, shrubs, vines or herbaceous plants. Some of these crops have multiple uses if they also provide essential oils for perfumes, dyes, or precursors to useful drugs for pharmaceutical purposes. Growing trees for timber is a separate part of this sector.

Ornamental horticulture occupies the niche left after subtracting plants with all these valuable attributes. In the modern era, flower growing has been industrialized and floral crops are now to be found in very large spaces such as fields or enclosed greenhouses. At one time, each country grew a wide variety of floral crops, but in the past two decades a move to more favorable climates and lower costs of labor has created a global but more restricted industry, with considerable specialization.

Countries in Central and South America, parts of Africa and some Middle Eastern countries have profited, while North American and Western European crops have decreased. In North America, some of the shift in the United States can be attributed to CAFTA (Central American Free Trade Agreement). Californian growers were particularly hard-hit. California, Florida, and Michigan lead the United States in floral output.

Ornamental horticulture is sufficiently large to be listed as a separate commercial category in the United States agricultural census since 1890. The census tracks numbers of potted plants and other measurable quantities, including the acreage allocated to ornamental horticulture and number of people employed.

## A Brief History of Horticulture in Germany

For centuries, there was no such country as "Germany," only a collection of German-speaking principalities and small states, loosely affiliated under the Holy Roman Emperor. Otto von Bismarck, the Kaiser's chief minister in the last quarter of the nineteenth century, was the force behind unifying all these small kingdoms in the 1870s, making sure that Prussia held the lead.

Germany lies on the North European Plain in the middle of Europe, largely landlocked without any extensive seaboard beyond a modest segment in the north opening onto the Baltic Sea and a really small strip along the North Sea. It thus has all the characteristics of a Continental climate: freezing cold winters and very hot summers. Crops grew adequately to support subsistence farming. The development of floriculture was a later refinement. The mass of the people in the early years were peasants living on the land. In most epochs, the country was self-sufficient in food, and some places were known for their vineyards and wine.

The other countries of Europe have varying access to the Atlantic Ocean, the North Sea, the Baltic Sea, and the Mediterranean Sea. These aspects of their geography together with their latitude affect their climate and thus horticultural production. Water surrounds the British Isles on all sides. The west coast of Britain has the added advantage of the Gulf Stream brushing its edges, warming the air temperature enough for flowers to blossom and vegetables to ripen there some weeks before the rest of the country. In really sheltered places like the Island of Tresco, off the coast of Cornwall, tropical plants can thrive. Nineteenth-century chrysanthemum breeders in Paris used to send their seedlings to the Island of Jersey in the English Channel to gain strength and bulk. There are very few such climatic havens in Germany.

MAP 2 Pre war Germany 1939

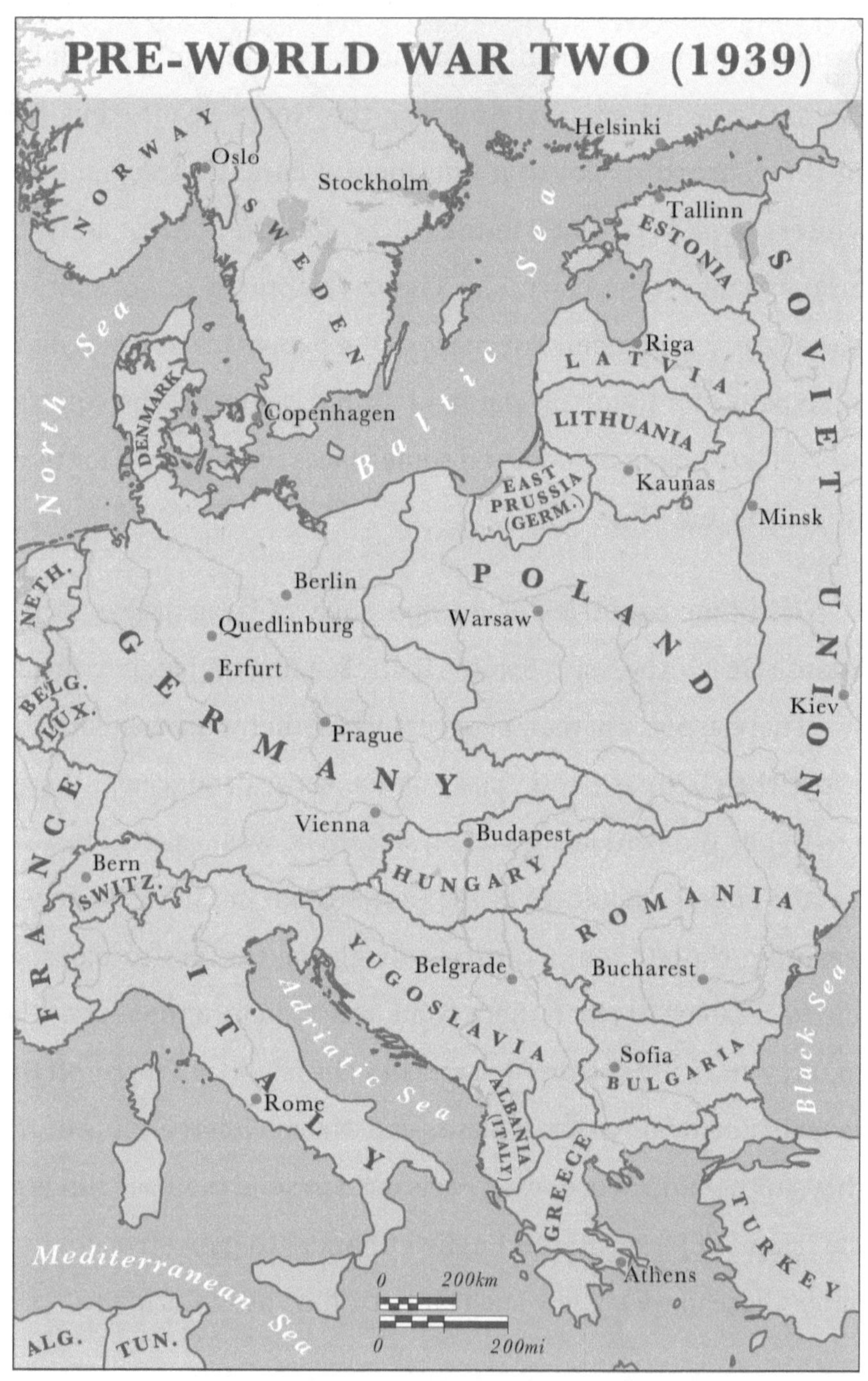

Horticulture developed across Germany in a very fragmented way. Wars disrupted life time and again. There were the Thirty-Year War which devastated Saxony-Anhalt, the Seven-Year War, the Napoleonic Wars, the Franco-Prussian War, the First World War, and finally the Second World War. It seemed that no sooner did the population try to get started again another war came along and destroyed everything. Please forgive me if I have left out any other wars to date. Oh yes, the Cold War.

The consequences of the wars of the twentieth century, especially WWII, were particularly bad for the sector of the country which became East Germany. After 1945, the Communist takeover of that territory increased the already extensive disruption and turmoil, not least in the horticulture and floriculture industry.

The first instructions came immediately. No one was allowed to grow flowers commercially. This was not all that unreasonable as orders go. For a long time, starting at the beginning of the world war and continuing into the postwar period, all available arable land had to be used to produce food.

German horticulture was very successful for centuries. As in all the other modern societies, it grew out of agriculture, because food was always the priority. Tracing the development of two significant cities, Erfurt and Quedlinburg, allows us to have some insight into how growing flowers *en masse* as a separate business happened. The purpose right from the start was to obtain seed.

When it comes to an overview of German horticulture we might as well start with Goethe. That is what Klaus Hoffmann did in his book. Johann Wolfgang von Goethe, 1749 – 1832, remains that ghastly untouchable figure, "a great cultural icon," in Germany and the Western world. His reputation rested on his writing: poetry, philosophy, politics, fiction, and scientific studies. The philosopher Arthur Schopenhauer considered Goethe's novel, *Wilhelm Meister,* to be one of the four greatest novels ever written. The other three were *La Nouvelle Heloise,* by Jean-Jacques Rousseau, *Tristram Shandy,* by Laurence Sterne, and Miguel Cervantes' *Don Quixote.* Few would quarrel with Schopenhauer's choices today, in spite of the great expansion of fiction in the last 150 years, but *Wilhelm Meister* may be gathering a bit more dust than *Tristram Shandy* and *Don Quixote.*

Part of the great reverence in which Goethe was held was that he also paid a lot of attention to the natural world around him. He lived during the "Age of Enlightenment," otherwise known as the "Age of Reason," and an educated person was expected to be conversant with science as well as art and literature. At that stage, it was still possible to encompass both types of study.

We can use Goethe's studies in botany to ground us in the world of European horticulture. His principal treatise on plants, *The Metamorphoses of Plants* (1790), which put him on the map scientifically, arose from a yearlong journey through Italy. Goethe suggested that plant structures were not fixed, but flexible and able to change with time and function, allowing the growth and development of leaves and blossom. He thought it possible that petals were a form of leaf, a concept which still has value today. Double flowers are possible because stamens can be converted into extra petals. Thorns are morphologically variants of leaves.

Goethe took a very close interest in his garden and dealt a lot with Herr Dreysigg, a nurseryman from Tonndorf near Weimar. Although Goethe belonged to the upper class and was an official at the Duke of Weimar's court, he respected this gardener a great deal and was willing to learn from him. Herr Dreyssig introduced Goethe to blue hydrangea, purple filled stock, georgien (dahlia), and auriculas over the years. Goethe's notebooks have really impressive drawings and descriptions of them.

Dahlias, as they are known in English, were only just becoming available at the end of the eighteenth century. Seeds went from Mexico City to Madrid at the end of the 18th century, and only after some years did the botanical garden in Madrid release them more widely. The confusion in the name was because two different taxonomists received specimens at roughly the same time. One named the plant "dahlia" for the Swedish botanist Anders Dahl. The other chose to name the plant "Georgina" and the plant was known by this name all over Europe. Eventually only the name "Dahlia" was used, even in Germany. In horticulture the very first name ever used takes precedence and dahlia came before georgina.

Goethe's friend, Alexander von Humboldt, traveled in South America from 1799 to 1805 and brought back seeds of miniature dahlias among his many other treasures.

Goethe's significance is that he straddled the epoch at which the intentional cross-breeding of new flowers was beginning to take hold. Plantsmen shrugged off the vague threats of the clerics that doing this interfered with God's prerogative as the sole creator of all things and would condemn to them to a long stretch in purgatory. Many of the most avid hybridizers were men of the cloth, such as Dean Herbert and Shirley Hibberd in England.

New plant introductions coincided with advances in the sciences at home. The sheer volume of hitherto unknown plants coming into Europe from many other places, as well as their power and beauty, led to a highly creative ferment. These experiments were being tried in England, France, and other countries, but as this book is about events in Germany and Eastern Europe those other breeders will not be mentioned further.

For a short period in the 1830s and 1840s, some flower breeders played it safe. They hesitated to challenge the religious believers head-on and gave their new creations vaguely authentic taxonomic names, suggesting a previously unknown species, not a new hybrid. The odd thing is that for centuries wealthy landowners had been crossing livestock quite openly to obtain better quality horses, sheep, and cattle, creating mules along the way and no one thought anything of it, yet when Thomas Fairchild crossed a carnation with a Sweet William in 1723 for the first time in recorded history, he crept around with a heavy burden of guilt for the rest of his life.

## Joseph Gottlieb Kölreuter

One of the earliest botanists to breed new flowers by intentional pollination in Germany was Joseph Gottlieb Kölreuter, 1733 – 1806. He worked with *Nicotiana rustica* and *N. panciculata* in the 1760s. This was forty years after Thomas Fairchild's experiment with a carnation in London.

Kölreuter had been professor of natural history in St Petersburg and curator of the Tsar's collection of fish. When he moved back to Germany, carefully carrying all his notes and specimens, he went to work for the margrave of Baden in Karlsruhe as professor of natural history and director of the palace gardens. Kölreuter had a profoundly scientific mind with its attendant curiosity, and no matter where he was he was always trying out new crosses between plants. In spite of the obvious inconvenience, he took his seedlings with him all the time.

The margrave's gardeners were still very conservative and pious and terrified of what Kölreuter was doing. While the margräfin Caroline was alive, Kölreuter had nothing to fear. She was interested in his work and protected him. The moment she died in 1786, the margrave sent Kölreuter packing. He had to give up his experimental work in the gardens but he was still able to lecture at the university.

Kölreuter has been largely forgotten except by specialists, but he was a direct forerunner of Gregor Mendel. He did bold experiments and thought widely about what he was trying to accomplish and what the results meant. He was a very careful observer and recorded his work in detail. Mendel also crossed different varieties of plant but his decision to count the offspring and treat the experiments mathematically is what makes Mendel immortal. He did it because he had studied statistics in Vienna as a student.

## Horticultural Training in Germany

Horticultural development in Middle Germany between the eighteenth and twentieth centuries was impressive. Many new nurseries sprang up as the demand for plants started taking off. This tremendous growth led to a need for good workers. It was heavy physical labor but quite rewarding if the gardener knew his plants. Urban nurseries became important employers but the days were long and the pay low.

The sole source of didactic information in Middle Germany until about the middle of the nineteenth century was Christian Reichart's writings. He codified information he had received from his father and other mentors as well what he had learned from his own experience. Information was handed down bot orally and in practical form. Formal training did not exist yet. Nurserymen who were able to travel abroad and visit nurseries in foreign countries brought back new things they had learned and applied them to their own work at home. In family businesses, parents taught their children.

A few men did have a proper education for their work. Ernst Benary, 1819 – 1893, was apprenticed to Haage & Schmidt. His friend and elementary school classmate, Franz Carl Heinemann, was trained at the Royal Belvedere garden in Weimar. Gustav Adolf Dippe spent three years in training with Martin Grashoff, and Christian Heinrich Mette learned about gardening and plants in the Quedlinburg cathedral gardens during his apprenticeship with Johann Heinrich Ziemann. These are just a few examples of prodigious nurserymen and more details about their lives will follow.

As the demand for plants increased, the old way just wasn't sufficient. Many horticultural societies tried to remedy this situation by offering free special training courses on Saturday evenings or during slow winter months. In 1838, Topf Nurseries in Erfurt started a private school offering basic and advanced courses in horticulture. The horticultural societies paid for these courses and experienced members offered to teach. In 1861 the Erfurt horticultural society "Flora" started holding teaching programs on specific topics.

Another "Flora," an offshoot of the Saxon Botany and Horticultural Society of Dresden founded in 1826, ran in parallel with the one in Erfurt. Right from the beginning it concentrated on botanical and horticultural education. The society constructed a special nursery for that purpose. This gave young trainees a practical starting point for a horticultural career. There were many other attempts to educate Saxon gardeners, but in most cases they didn't amount to much.

Some fifty years later, Saxony switched to an apprentice system. The state funded it at first and people thought all the problems had been solved. Alas, that was not to be. The support was withdrawn. At the same time, there were many different views on what kind of training was needed – practical or theoretical. Finally it became clear that education and training for horticulture as a profession needed to be combined into one field of study, whether in Thüringia, Saxony, Saxony-Anhalt, or Berlin.

The national association of German horticulture led the way in 1930. The association laid out the program and only certified institutions would be recognized. This marked the beginning of current horticultural vocational training. More recently it has become possible to specialize after finishing the basic course. An apprentice can go into nursery stock sales and marketing, plant growing and propagation, ornamental plant or perennial cultivation, arboriculture, seed production, cemetery horticulture, landscaping, or floristry. This is still a model for horticultural training, but has been modified over time to take account of changes.

Erfurt established its own program in 1848. Some years later, Hans Settegast, a well- known horticulturist of that era, founded an agricultural school in Rudolstadt in 1878. Subsequently, he started a similar school in Bad Koestritz which later became part of another horticultural institution. He was named professor in 1909 and remained as the director for forty-seven years. (As an aside, John McLaren reigned over San Francisco's Golden Gate Park for the same period of time.)

Quedlinburg set up a research program to test agricultural machinery in 1933. The leaders of the DDR constantly expanded this place. At one point it became a residential school with a huge greenhouse. The DDR establishment relied on it completely.

The agricultural department of Berlin's Humboldt University played an important role in the establishment of horticulture in the 20th century. It worked with a special school in nearby Moeglin founded by Albrecht Daniel Thaer (1752-1828), an early scientist and teacher who published many papers on botany, zoology, chemistry, geology, and mathematics. He was buried in Moeglin, where he is honored by a museum and a monument. Erwin Bauer and Kurt von Ruemmker made significant contributions to the growing field of horticulture and landscape design up until the beginning of the Nazi era.

**History and value of garden shows**

Trade shows had a very positive and direct effect on innovation and sales. All the new plant and flower varieties sold best when the customers could see them for themselves.

Businesses got together and organized these shows, which in turn led to the formation of horticultural societies.

The Erfurter Gartenbau Verein (Erfurt Horticultural Society) (EGV) was founded in 1838 and the Erfurter Handelsgaertner (Market Gardener) Society in 1883. The members of the EGV decided to put together a show. Each plant would be individually identified with a tag. Visitors would be able to see all the plants and to ask questions about growing requirements, etc.

The first Erfurt Plant Show was held in 1840 and became a tradition. The show was repeated twice a year, spring and fall, so that beautiful seasonal plants could be displayed. Fall dahlias became very popular not only in Erfurt but also in many other Thuringian towns, as well as other places. (114) Seventy-two of the hundred and twenty-two exhibitors at the 1861 show were from Erfurt. 1865 was the first year of international participation at the Erfurt Plant Show. In 1871 Thuringian and Saxon nurseries created a special combined plant show. (24)

Participation in international shows was important and possible for the big companies up until 1960. They displayed azaleas, camellias and rhododendron and also showed blooming one-year-old plants for cutting and potted plants. All this was crucial for their export business. More recently, there have not been many plant shows in Saxony-Anhalt except for small regional plant exhibits and some sightseeing in Quedlinburg growing grounds.

After World War Two, horticultural exports stopped completely. Everything was needed urgently inside the country. Plant shows began again later. There was one on the grounds of the Erfurt Cyriaksburg in 1950 called "Erfurt blueht" (Erfurt in Bloom), and one for seeds, again in Erfurt called "Erfurter Samen-Export Schau" in 1955.

Starting in 1961, co-operative nurseries and horticulturists were able to present their wares annually in Erfurt and Markleeberg. It was also possible to offer plants in Dresden's Fucikplatz and under Berlin's television tower. The character of the exhibits had changed. Instead of sharing information and expertise, exhibitors were required to focus on themes such as playgrounds and small gardens, all part of a strategy to use horticulture to influence society. Kristina Vagt has written a very useful book on this topic, the use of the flower shows made by politicians to boost their own government's point of view in what should have been neutral scientific and floricultural displays.

Cleaning up the ruins left by the Soviet occupation led to remarkable results in all three DDR states. Beautiful displays were to be seen in the Thuringian towns of Poessneck and

Nordhausen. Both in Saxony-Anhalt and in Saxony itself, the towns of Zeitz, Aschersleben, Wernigerode, Zittau, and Lichtenstein all held shows which led to parks and gardens being built. There were also state garden shows in Cottbus, Magdeburg and Gera/Ronneburg.

## Marketing

The rapid introduction of new cultivars by nineteenth and twentieth century Middle German nurserymen made sales and marketing key. In the beginning, this was limited to the local nurseries that sold their own plants or cut flowers on site. At first, they sold seeds in little bags. Eventually, specialized seed dealers started buying the seeds in bulk and then repackaged them for retail sales.

The other opportunity to sell their plants was at local markets. This was difficult because it entailed carting fragile goods over bad roads in unpredictable weather and the difficulties of loading and unloading a large number of plants. Buyers wanted to be able to see the plants the nurseries had to offer. Soon the bigger producers started making lists of their cultivars, using their common German names at first. That led to organizing the plant lists by colors or shapes, and even by plant use. Finally, botanical names were used.

New definitions were required for the hybrids which, starting at the beginning of the nineteenth century, resulted in the use of the term "variety." In time a product list, later a "variety list," was no longer sufficient so the bigger companies started printing catalogues to cover all their new cultivars.

Vegetable varieties were treated the same way. With all the new varieties of plants produced annually, the big companies had to keep updating their catalogues. Catalogues became important marketing instruments for selling seeds and seedlings. The mutual effect of product development and sales resulted in greater consumer interest and increased production—in today's slang, "a win-win situation."

## Chapter 2 Agriculture and horticulture in East Germany (Deutsche Demokratische Republik DDR)

The government of East Germany had only one goal: destroy the existing order as quickly as possible and create a Socialist paradise. They used a two-pronged approach. One was by directly confiscating land and businesses. The other was by creating such burdensome requirements to continue in business that many simply threw up their hands and closed down, releasing more property for the state.

A handy way to get the process started was to accuse large companies of serving Nazism and therefore helping in the war. Mishandling Jews or prisoners of war or cooking the books was another set of crimes, enabling the new authorities to dispossess the owners and nationalize their businesses without any compensation. This was pretty rich coming from the Stalinist regime, which rounded up Jews only slightly less happily than Hitler. There was no due process and no appeal.

In the very early period, 1945 to 1946, many owners and their senior employees managed to leave everything in time and flee to the West, mainly to West Germany. They could not take any money or possessions with them and also forfeited all claims to their property. If they were lucky, they had friends or family who helped them to start again.

Once they had gone, the authorities went into high gear. Soviet military command #58 stated, for example, that all agricultural corporations larger than a hundred hectares needed to be nationalized. The owners didn't just lose the land, but also all the buildings and their inventory as well as their money. The proceeds of all this went into a fund to be divided between agricultural laborers, evacuees, and small farmers.

This was an intermediate step not previously considered necessary but had to be done in the DDR to reach the next level. That goal was full collectivization of the land. Because of this move, thousands of tiny farms came into being, each with fewer than ten hectares—highly inefficient under any regime, but for a short time it fed the desire for land among a repressed peasantry.

A formerly landless laborer seemed ready for a leg up. The major problems such people faced were the lack of living quarters, stalls, machines, animals, and seeds, and above all, skilled workers to assist them. There was one bright spot. The new farmers were able to make use of the former owners' buildings by recycling the materials.

On the other hand, a poor, uneducated man accustomed always to working for another person seldom learned how to take charge and work things out for himself. The responsibility was too great for many of them and they were unable to take proper advantage of this new situation. It needed a capacity for abstract thought and planning ahead they lacked. The much maligned "kulaks" in Russia became kulaks precisely because they had these abilities. As has so often been the case in huge upheavals, under the high-flown rhetoric, people also used the situation to settle ancient scores. Jealousy and resentment were usually the prevailing motives.

During this phase, about thirty percent of the arable land was used to set up state-owned farms, VEG. VEG is the acronym for Volkseigenes Gut, a people-owned (i.e. state- owned) entity. The state appointed the directors of the VEGs. The workers had absolutely no say in their functions. In contrast, committees of workers controlled the LPGs: Landwirtschaftliche Produktionsgenossenschafte (Agricultural Collective)—at least in theory. The principal feature of all these arrangements was that almost no actual money went to workers. All cash accrued to the state.

At first, the VEGS produced animals, plants, and seed to supply the LPGs. By 1960, there were 690 such organizations. The numbers fell because of increasing specialization in agriculture and horticulture and resulting mergers. For example, cattle raising would separate from dairy farming and then groups of cattle raisers formed one organization and the dairy farmers another. As this process of forming the collectives was underway, the leaders decreed that animal husbandry should be separated from arable farming.

Klaus Hoffmann commented in his book that the VEGS were treated better than the LPGs. The latter were starved of capital and equipment. This led to fatalism and complete loss of morale on the part of the workers: why bother? The failure was so abysmal that the DDR had to import food for a period of time.

The large companies no longer existed, but if a firm owned fewer than a hundred hectares it was allowed to continue as an independent operator, at least for the short term. At that stage, the entire agricultural sector, including nurseries, was coerced into producing food. They were not permitted to grow anything else. Because of unrealistic targets, set by Moscow, difficulties emerged right from the start: not enough potatoes, too much cabbage, and problems like that. Was anyone allowed to grow onions?

The second wave of the destruction of the agricultural companies came through the burden of the planned requirements. The arbitrariness of the interpretation of the regulations was intended for the larger companies that had managed to survive. Imaginary charges of fraud, deception, graft, hoarding and actions against the socialist government were used as justifications for the penalties of fines and imprisonment.

Many nurserymen and remaining horticulturists, for example Alfred Heinemann, were imprisoned or kidnapped. In 1951, the Ernst Benary firm was convicted of white-collar crime *in absentia.*

About 3.8 million people fled the DDR before it officially became a state in 1949. This was almost twenty percent of the total population. The departure of so many people affected those remaining very badly. The first General Secretary of the DDR Communist Party, the SED, from 1950, Walter Ulbricht (1893-1973), was concerned about the loss of so many educated workers. Unlike other Communist leaders who feared the influence of educated people, he realized how important they were for the country to succeed. There were towns with no teachers or doctors, for instance. An additional 3.1 million left between 1949 and 1960. One can regard these departures as the people voting with their feet. The last remaining route to leave East Germany via Berlin was sealed off when the infamous wall was built in 1961.

Ignoring this reality and regardless of what it cost, the government was going to establish "the first socialist state on German soil." The eventual goal was to demonstrate that socialist methods led to greater productivity and prosperity than the old capitalist ones. The way they implemented this program was more of the same, only in an increasingly concentrated form. There was a greater push to collectivize and to create more VEBs (Publicly-Owned Firms) in agriculture and horticulture.

In spite of this rhetoric, the change to fully nationalized businesses was gradual. In the beginning, The first seed that became available was from the old private businesses. There was no other source. As the process moved forward, some firms were more adept at dealing with seed while others dealt largely in vegetative plants.

Increasing the means of production was essential, but the method, by "voluntary force," whatever that meant, was primarily politically motivated. The affected companies had no way out. Agricultural Production Cooperatives, Landwirstschaftliche Produktionsgenossneschaft, (LPG) began in 1953. A little later Horticultural Production Cooperatives, Gartnerischen Produktiongenossneschaft (GPG) got going.

The basis of the LPG's formation was the so-called formerly Russian "model statutes." There were different types of cooperatives, but the collectivization of agriculture was enforced through party and state power, often with threats and violence. This hollowed out the principle of voluntary "Leninist cooperative planning." No one dared ask any questions.

With this grim background, it seems almost frivolous to consider what happened to floriculture. Total collectivization was supposed to be completed by 1960. From some of the records and according to Hoffmann, this goal was honored more in the breach. A local leader would report that he had met his goal whereas in fact he had not done it yet. Such men held their breath and prayed no one would come to inspect their region. If officials did show up, they did not want to hear about any problems or the fates of individuals.

Once Erich Honecker, 1912–1994, took over as first secretary of the SED (Sozialistische Einheitspartei Deutschlands), in 1971, there was continuing pressure to concentrate the smaller groups into larger collectives, divided between animal and field crop production. Honecker was more rigidly doctrinaire than Walter Ulbricht, the previous first secretary. Several cooperative communities or cooperative divisions came into being, including KAP (Cooperative Department of Plant Production), ACZ (Agrochemical Center), and ZBE (Interfirm Organization). The results were mixed. Excuses about the division of labor, the size of the firm or the division of horticulture, agriculture and animal husbandry were common rationales given for weak performance.

In horticulture, the pressure to develop GPGs, Gärtnerischen Produktionsgenossenschafte, (Horticultural Cooperatives), similar to those in agriculture, was significant, although it made little sense for many nurseries. As the end product was not a monocrop for mass distribution, the flower industry did not lend itself to the sweeping modifications required. Once the authorities got rid of the very large well-run floricultural businesses, countless nurseries tacitly remained as small family operations. The existing cooperatives saw no value in adding any of these seemingly rundown or unproductive nurseries, where the war had taken a huge toll.

The fact that up until 1989 there was still a large number of private nurseries shows that in this area collectivization was not particularly well-managed. Many private companies, including the nurseries, were quite successful during the DDR, more so than later in the market economy. The reasons for the failure to continue to be successful were manifold, such as inadequate production and an inability to set prices for the products due to lack of experience. These modest firms were able to coast under the old system but fell very short in a different one.

The owners of land and other property could only reclaim it after 1989 if they could establish their ownership, and then as long as no one else could produce title. The state invested early in F.C. Heinemann and N.L. Chrestensen, both large companies. In 1961, the state offered them more financial assistance in exchange for acting as a "silent partner." This was a very hypocritical move, but what could they do? Better to have involvement by the state than lose the company entirely.

The decisive year was 1972. The last large private horticultural business was nationalized but the company wasn't taken off the land register. Only a few exceptions were made for companies to continue to operate privately, for example the

Engler Firm in Miltitz near Leipzig and the P.J. Schmidt Firm in Quedlinburg. Klaus Hoffmann could not understand why they were allowed to do this. Looking back with the 20:20 vision of hindsight, I think it is possible that financial emoluments for the relevant officials involved might have played a role.

Sometimes a cooperative sold the property, often together with its members. A private sale through the owners was not possible, even though the owners' names were never stricken from the title register. Owners were only compensated when the state needed the land for important construction and transportation projects—to create allotments for citizens, railroad track, etc.—and then with pennies on the dollar.

After reunification, official cooperatives could continue operating, albeit under new laws laid down in accordance with the rules of the Federal Republic of Germany as well as the content of the Unification Treaty of 1990. The decision of the members for or against this path was binding. A few made an effort to continue, but it was an untenable situation. There was no way they could survive in the new climate.

There were a lot of obstacles for the continued existence of cooperatives. Sloppy, haphazard practices meant that greenhouses, hothouses, and storage buildings had been built on pieces of land belonging to many different owners. Building permits were ignored. If a member of the cooperative resigned, perhaps a nursery remained but didn't have a hothouse, or their greenhouse was on land belonging to someone else. In the midst of this confusion, new land registry documents were written up based on "special rules" stipulated in the Unification Treaty. All this made it simply impossible to continue a company or to take it private.

## Measuring the effects

The correct way to measure the effects of a major change in policy is to establish output before and after the disruption occurred. How many ornamental plants were grown and sold in Germany and the Eastern European countries in the 1930s before World War II and how many were sold afterwards? This deceptively simple and logical approach works very well for well-run economies with a tradition of monitoring output in the various sectors.

Trying to apply this logic in post-World War II Europe is another matter. Even assuming that before the war careful records were kept, the turmoil of the immediate prewar years and the actual war, plus the catastrophic ruination which the war left in its wake militate against the possibility of any useful records surviving. Many German buildings were reduced to rubble. Eighty percent of the city center of Berlin was destroyed. Dresden was devastated as were many other smaller German towns.

Some of the capital cities of Eastern Europe escaped damage, notably Prague and Riga, but Warsaw was reduced to ruin after a short siege in 1939. Budapest also suffered considerable damage. It depended on whether the warring parties believed there was strategic value in bombing them. In Romania, Bucharest was not as badly hit as Ploesti, the oil center. Parts of Lithuania were pulverized.

Valuable public records were burned or destroyed in the aftermath of the bombing and fighting. At that point, no one was remotely concerned about matters of tertiary importance such as horticultural output. All anyone wanted to do was find food and shelter.

It is entirely likely that small numbers of flowers were still being grown in the relatively undamaged regions of Germany for use in funerals and perhaps a few weddings. During the war, Benary in Erfurt removed all its ornamental plants and grew potatoes and cabbage for the German forces. The latter obligingly turned a blind eye to the business's Jewish origins.

Once the Socialists were toppled and a market economy of sorts was in effect, the sluggishness and almost total breakdown of the previous system became clear. Bokelmann and Lentz reported that in the ten years between 1990 and 2000, East German fruit production fell by 80%, vegetable production fell by about 85%, and the production of ornamental plants dropped by about 80%. Dehnen-Schmutz and her colleagues commented that these numbers indicate just how disconnected Eastern European agriculture was from that in the West.

Many privately owned horticultural firms had remained open during the occupation but did not have the resources to keep up production under market conditions. The horticultural cooperatives in the DDR were larger than the family-owned businesses but they lacked sufficient capital and were saddled with obsolescent machinery and old-fashioned techniques which led to lower productivity. The reunification of Germany allowed the former DDR to move forward, away from these disadvantages. The few prescient nurserymen who had transferred their businesses to West Germany very soon after the Russians moved in ran parallel firms until the reunification. Merging them was not too difficult.

Today, in other Eastern European countries there has been a rebound of sorts. Communist meddling interfered with existing business, but structural reforms combined with lower costs for labor in poorer countries have allowed progress to be made. Many of these countries have now joined the EU.

**Chapter 3: Methods used to transform East Germany's agricultural sector**

In February 1946, the Soviet military authorities in control of the Eastern sector of Germany, SBZ, issued order number 58, mandating the restoration of seed cultivation for agricultural crops. To set things going, the Soviet Military Administration of Germany ordered the establishment of the German Seed Association, Pflanzenzuchtung und Saatgutwirtschaft zentral (DSG) in 1946. This institution was responsible for all regulations controlling new varieties and cultivars, the seed-breeding process, business regulations for the seed breeding companies, and the processing and distribution of seeds. None of that was a simple matter.

All expropriated seed producing companies were obliged to participate in the DSG, including the E. Benary Firm in 1952, parts of F.C. Heinemann, and most of the seed growing companies in Quedlinburg and surrounding area. Almost an entire branch of the economy was now owned by the state. Heinemann was finally fully nationalized in 1972.

Agricultural seed production and growing the plants for seed production, combined with plant breeding, were separated from the trading of seeds. The formation of the VEG (State Owned Farm)-Seeds and the nationally-owned DSG district companies went on simultaneously. Hoffmann found it all quite bewildering, as companies seemed to multiply. (The author (JMT) apologizes for the continued multiplication of acronyms. It was a feature of the times.)

Up until 1963 the seed developing organization was attached to the Ministry of Agriculture but then became independent. It was called the VEB (people-owned enterprise) Seed and Seeding Materials, and was managed by a chief executive officer. Its headquarters were in Quedlinburg. New regulations came pouring out. The directors were dissatisfied with the results of contemporary breeding and trading but the poor performance was hardly surprising given the circumstances.

Ornamental plants were dealt with later through what Hoffmann termed "special operations." A VEG Seed Production for Ornamental Plants was formed in Erfurt and was made up of twelve operating sections, distributed over the entire DDR. This entity was responsible for the production of seeds and seeding materials, the export of their products, and for the breeding itself. The responsibilities of the VEB Seed and Seeding Materials were unbelievably large.

This required growers to set up an association of seed growers with branches in several cities, the DSG, Deutsche Samen Geschaft (German Seed Society). By June 1946, Edwin Hoernie, the chief administrator of the department of agriculture and forestry, signed an official decree laying out the governance, acquisition, and distribution of seeds and all relevant plant material. This decree legalized a process which had started in the autumn of 1945, when the Russian occupiers began seizing the property of large landholders. The excuse was that the owners had collaborated with the Nazis. The DSG operated until 1950. After that, the Academy of Agricultural Sciences, with its institutes for cultivation, became responsible for breeding new varieties.

The Seeding Material and Seeds VEB in Quedlinburg had to maintain cultivation and production. It was also responsible for certifying seed, to be certain it would perform as claimed. The proportion of certified seed grew from 20% in 1950 to almost 100% by 1980. Much of the work assigned to this organization lay in educating growers to understand the influence of local conditions on plant performance.

It may not be an exaggeration to say that Germany, post-World War II, was close to famine in some places. The necessity to get food production going and to have enough seed to do that was imperative. During the war, Germany had commandeered food from the countries it occupied. The Germans had ruined the economies of the eastern territories it had conquered and decimated their populations. They had no food to export to Germany. They were barely surviving themselves. After the war, no one was ready to help Germany until President Truman sent Herbert Hoover to take charge of getting food flowing around Europe again. Hoover was a consummate administrator and had done the same thing after World War One.

Waiting for seeds to provide a crop takes a minimum of a year. The obvious solution of importing food, given the conditions noted above, was highly unlikely. Presumably Hoover found pockets of food stock and was able to start things moving again. Few countries had any food to spare except for North America and the neutral lands of Sweden Switzerland, Eire and some parts of the British Commonwealth, nor was there any spare seed to be had worldwide. In the midst of such a catastrophe, flower seeds were not even mentioned. Their production re-emerged some years later.

## Taking control: rules for growing new flowers

Growing ornamental plants again began in the 1960s. The Ministry of Agriculture set up a state holding company in 1963, the VEB, Volkseigenes Betrieb, a "people–owned" enterprise, to manage all this, with headquarters in Quedlinburg. In a few years, its responsibilities spread further across the rest of the DDR. Only the very small nurseries and the few individuals who bred flowers as a hobby were exempt from being swept up into the VEB.

The surviving old nurseries were in terrible shape. Working with the dilapidated cold frames was backbreaking toil. Popular old-fashioned flowers like petunia, begonia, cineraria, and heliotrope are labor-intensive and were very hard to grow in large quantities, but politics always complicated even the simplest decisions such as renovation.

It was decided that the smallest nurseries should be combined into larger units. The theory behind amalgamating the tiny businesses was laudable. The state wanted to introduce better crops and shorten the time required to breed new cultivars by collaboration and the exchange of primary genetic material. What actually happened was almost exactly the reverse. If one wanted to devise a method for stultifying imagination and creativity, then the DDR floriculture industry is the model. Underpinning all the arrangements was the terrifying need for order without loose ends, referred to earlier. Very few, if any, human activities lend themselves to this.

Professor Gerhard Roebbelen laid out the way this system was supposed to operate. Horticulturists could only work with designated plants approved by the Ministry of Agriculture, Forestry, and Food Commodities Industry. The names of certified varieties of herbaceous plants were published by the ZfS (Central Office for Variety Registration), every two years. The list for perennial plants and blossoming trees came out every five years. If the license to grow any particular plant were revoked, the list indicated how long the revocation lasted and what its replacement would be. This tight control on output was maintained even for plants intended solely for export.

Deciding on which plants to grow and who would be allowed to do that was carried out by committees and working groups which met frequently and visited nurseries at least once. The bar for introducing a new variety was very high. A new plant had to be better than any foreign plants, based on analyses of the literature. If it did not reach that standard, then it had at least to be equivalent to them or *en route* to reach that level. There was strong pressure to place everything in the first category.

Perfectionist standards of this sort led to more problems. If the grower were to reach the same level as a foreign business, it was necessary to obtain source material from abroad. Given the abysmal balance of payments in the DDR, there was not enough currency to do that most of the time. Not only that, but growers had very limited access to the literature they would need to carry out the work. Free access to knowledge threatened the hierarchy's control. The only exception was if a grower had connections in another socialist country.

If someone received the green light to go ahead, they almost immediately had to supply enough seeds and seedlings to get the plant into production. Crystal balls and tea leaves got a good workout. It was a terrible gamble for the breeder, whether to bulk up a not-yet-certified crop just in case it were accepted. If a really small grower were to receive the nod, in general it made more sense to sell the whole production to one of the larger organizations and not even try to carry it out. The larger VEGS could absorb the cost of growing the new variety out of its lump sum payment from the state each year.

Once the committee agreed on what was to be grown, the next step was to set the price. That price was the same no matter who the grower was or where it was grown. Because the price took no account of local conditions and costs, many approved new varieties never got grown or sold. Even if the price of a new variety had to be higher, there also had to be constant price balance between the groups of new and old. It was safer to stick to older kinds, which were well understood. The need for a fixed price ignored the obvious major variables in any plant-based business.

One of the largest factors was labor costs: the number and quality of permanent workers, the need for seasonal workers, and where and how the seasonal workers could be obtained. The best source of seasonal workers was a country with far lower levels of income whose citizens would work for much less money than the East Germans. Poland was a good source and occasionally countries further east. Even seasonal workers need a modicum of training, and that is an investment of time and effort which has to be considered.

Then came energy costs: East Germany lacked much in the way of endemic energy other than brown lignite coal. Higher quality coal, natural gas, and oil all had to be imported. In an ordinary economy, fluctuations in these costs would be reflected in the price. Heating a greenhouse in a cold country like Germany, even with the best energy conservation practices possible, is very expensive. Imported fuel was also subject to tariffs which also affected the cost.

The cost of the land usually has a big impact on price as well, but not in this case. The DDR had simply stolen the land from the previous owners without paying for it.

Finally, there were water, pesticides, and fertilizers. Water was not an issue in the East German plant-growing cities, close as they were to large rivers. Pesticides and fertilizers were essential in producing a healthy crop and had to be bought, no matter what.

Color, fragrance, early blossoming, ability to bloom for a longer time, resistance to disease—all characteristics which would drive demand—did not enter into it. If this sounds like "voodoo" economics, it is because it was. There was the reverse of an incentive to innovate. Because of this rigidity—and hence timidity—the growers found it very difficult to meet specific deadlines like International Women's Day on March 8, even with old favorites such as tulips, narcissus, and hyacinth.

The authorities thought they wanted innovation and gave awards for it when it happened. As no one lost money for failing to deliver, so neither did anyone make much money for doing better than the norm. Sometimes it was possible to hybridize a cultivar quietly which met the criteria for an official one from the ZfS sufficiently without having to go through the complicated process of licensing a new introduction.

Naming was another minefield. If they did manage to bring in a new plant from the West, the name had to be changed. The DDR could not allow a plant called 'President Kennedy' or 'Lili Marlene' to be released. Once in a while, there was the little matter of an existing foreign trademark. It is hard to reconcile all these unpleasant realities with the excellent research that was going on behind the scenes.

Producing seed was always most important, but an increasing demand for young starter plants began. This demand led to further specialization in horticulture. Most of the old infrastructure for seeds remained in use. It was clumsy and needed a lot of manpower. Producing some of the popular old-fashioned flowers like petunia, begonia, cineraria, and heliotrope was very hard work.

The Institute for Ornamental Horticulture at the Humboldt University began research on improving vegetative methods of propagation in 1953. Roses and chrysanthemums were some of the first plants they tackled. Some of the problems they needed to solve were the use of in-vitro generation and the fact that mixing genes from two different species was very difficult, creating a barrier to inter-specific hybridization, and making mutation work for them. To complete the Kafka-esque nature of these organizations, the results of this research were not allowed to be published.

As firms ramped up the production of seedlings, they had to protect the vulnerable young plants from viral infections. The VEG PAC Plants Dresden did some of the most valuable work, particularly with chrysanthemums. Pelargoniums are also very susceptible to viral infestation.

Two major botanical institutions in Crimea were allowed to share in this research, the Institute for Ornamental Plants at Sochi and the Nikitski Botanical Garden at Yalta. The Nikitski Botanical Garden had great expertise in clematis. (see *An Abundance of Flowers*) This was all done through intermediaries. The scientists were not allowed to communicate with each other.

Poland was another partner. The Institute for Fruit and Ornamental Plants at Skierniewice, plus a few other smaller places, corresponded with their coevals in the DDR. Some East German scientists were allowed to attend conferences. The Poles were working on disease prevention, particularly fungi in China asters, *Callistephus*.

The authorities had a similar relationship with Czechoslovakia. Equivalent institutions at Pruhonice and Semex worked with the university on begonia and snapdragon (*Antirrhinum*). This was more successful, albeit very late in the trajectory for the DDR. The political clock had started to run down. Seven varieties of the snapdragon series 'Start 82' were introduced in the DDR between 1982 and 1990. In Hungary they collaborated with their counterparts in Budapest on rust-resistant hollyhocks (*Alcea*).

All this was very nice, but in the end the East Germans had to rely on themselves and their own material for the majority of any new plants being introduced. Foreign material was sparse and insufficient for wider distribution. When the resulting new seedlings reached Quedlinburg and Berlin, they did not thrive in local conditions. It was all a waste.

Dresden was a center for azalea (*Rhododendron*) as well as pelargoniums. Rhododendron had always done well in Germany. Hans Hachmann of Barnstedt and Dietrich Hobbie near Hamburg were renowned breeders and growers of rhododendron in spite of the brutal winters in those regions. A number of new rhododendrons was also introduced by Mittendorf in Burg in 1976 and 1977. Two more valuable cultivars came from Daenhardt: 'Golden Rider' and 'Flamingo.' Albrecht introduced 'Merula' in 1989. The master of the dahlia, Christian Keegen, had worked in Bad Kostritz and his lines were continued there.

Graduates of the Humboldt University Department of Horticulture could expect to go into good jobs with the nationalized nurseries. They provided one bright spot in what was otherwise a rather dire situation. At least they knew the basics and could make more informed decisions.

## Nursery reconstruction

Eventually, the government allowed the VEB (Volkseigenes Betrieb, "People–owned" enterprise") management to reconstruct some of the premises. As noted earlier the aging nurseries had become very dilapidated. Accomplishing goals set down by rules and regulation for production and the associated system of inspection and reporting in such rundown premises was hard. Much of what was produced was distributed around Thuringia. Some part of this stock went abroad, while the potted plants primarily stayed in and around the two major cities. In 1968, construction began on a new greenhouse facility in Mittelhausen, within the city limits of Erfurt. It was finished ten years later. They constructed seventeen hectares of glass panels and four hectares of polytunnel buildings on inferior arable land. A thousand square meters of glass panels or polytunnels and five thousand square meters of open land were used to create new cultivars.

Agricultural buildings and social buildings came next. They installed a system for long-distance heating (tapping into waste heat from industrial plants and moving it to the nurseries), a large workshop complex, and a four-story administrative and social building with one floor for assistants' rooms and another as a dormitory for apprentices. There were about seventy apprentices each year.

Two laboratories were also built, one for soil research and the other for breeding plants under sterile conditions. The administrative building also had a medical station that could be used at any time by any of the 350 workers and a kitchen with a dining area. In addition, they also built a daycare center that could also be used by the neighboring communities. During peak seasons, they needed additional help. There could be up to a hundred temporary workers, often students from Poland or Czechoslovakia. A large part of the ornamental plant production was earmarked for export.

The construction of this complex was triggered by many factors. There was not enough greenhouse space in the Erfurt VEG to produce all the required potted plants and seedlings. The production of ornamental plants and vegetables for the Erfurt area tended to be seen as a question of prestige though the need to increase exports for the DDR's economy was really more important. With this, what was then the large investment of eighty million marks was justified. The result was that about 80 million chrysanthemum, geranium, dianthus, and euphorbia seedlings, along with about one and half million cut flowers and a million potted orchids and other plants, were produced.

The employees were very proud of "their" operation. It used modern methods, almost an oxymoron in the DDR. They made constant efforts to improve workflow and increase production as best they could. The scientific leader at the time, R. Kadner and a number of employees are still active today in the Leibniz Institute of Grossbeeren/Kuehnhausen as directors or research scientists. The current Institute was created after the construction of the Greenhouse Facility Mittelhausen was complete. It was built between 1985 and 1988 and was seen as a scientific center for the entire Erfurt area.

The number of permanent workers in the Greenhouse Facility Mittelhausen seems large, but low productivity was a generic problem in the DDR. Some of this was the lack of any useful mechanization. Mainly it was lack of motivation. Anything approaching "technology" had to be built by the workshop itself. There were no potting machines, for example. Each pot was filled by hand. Tractor-trailers brought bark from the Thuringia forest to prepare pots for orchids three months every year.

**Ornamental Plant Product Group in the DDR**

Naturally there had to be an Ornamental Plant Product Group: an EZG, (Erzeugergemeinshchaften). Such organizations were *de rigeur* in socialist countries. It was an agglomeration of horticultural businesses subdivided into fourteen sub-product groups (EZUs) and three different work groups. The businesses were already incorporated into VEGs and GPGs (horticultural collectives). With only a few exceptions, private companies were excluded. The exceptions were for orchids, cacti and woody plants. In those cases, the only ones who knew anything much about such plants were the leaders of private companies. Many of the member companies and their specialists were involved with several EZUs. All of this took an enormous amount of time away from their real work at the nurseries.

An EZU was primarily political, a panel of experts who operated under the Quedlinburg VEB for seed and seed stock and also under the director of the VEG for ornamental plants in Erfurt. Each of the fourteen subgroups: roses, dianthus, chrysanthemums, gerbera, orchids, anthurium, cut flowers, perennials, freesia, woody plants, leafy plants, potted plants, cyclamen, pelargonium, and cacti and other succulents, in addition to foliage, bromeliads, and gesneriads, had its own leader. These subgroup managers were usually experienced nurserymen or graduate students at the Humboldt University in Berlin or the horticultural school in Dresden. A full-time coordinator was in charge of all the EZG related work.

Apart from the busy work, the purpose was to coordinate and streamline production, and, as was so often the case, tie up loose ends. The idea was to prevent the rough and tumble of an open market which functions pretty well when left to itself. The panel was bound to follow political rules, having to set up socialist party conventions, agricultural party congresses, and similar responsibilities. Its main task was to meet the population's demand for high quality plants and cut flowers, especially for events like International Women's Day.

The EZG's advisory board set out new goals every year. These so-called business plans always included a professionally pertinent goal, but everything else was political. This was shrugged off as a necessary evil. The EZUs were supposed to evaluate and compare the economic health of the member businesses and then discuss the results. This was a pretty miserable job and very unpopular, since there were no guidelines for such evaluations. In that sort of vacuum, personality and settling of old scores could play a role.

The advisory board met for two days a few times a year. It was useful as a place to exchange information otherwise difficult to come by in a closed system of economic scarcity and political oppression. The members shared what they had learned about new plant varieties and the results of certain research projects, especially when information was brought back by the few members who had been able to make professional trips abroad. The importance of these good collegial relationships and information exchange which extended beyond the organized meetings is not to be underestimated. The EZUs dissolved with reunification.

**The environment**

East Germany was not known for its tenderness toward the environment. Rushing to industrialize and extract the maximum possible from their natural resources, such niceties as worrying about the health of the forest was not high on their list. Arvid Nelson points out in his excellent *Cold War Ecology* that the enormous abuse of forest land was a clear indication of the rate at which the economy was declining. Unopposed clearcutting left the land without protection or renewal.

Marxist-Leninist dialectic held that man was at constant war with nature. The natural world was to be used as man saw fit at that moment, with no thought for its continuation and renewal in the future. This view strongly resembles that of the Bible, an amusing irony for a supposedly religion-free society. Karl Marx could not escape his upbringing in a nineteenth century family and saw no further than his nose. It also happens to be the rapacious philosophy of many modern capitalists: extract, extract, extract. Even the most benighted aristocrat in the eighteenth century knew better. Owners of great estates planted trees which they knew they would never see fully grown during their lifetime but which were essential for the good of the property.

Erich Honecker had replaced Walter Ulbricht as general secretary of the Communist Party and thus leader of the DDR. He was a purist and could not tolerate the slightest bit of diversity in his vision of the country. That included the forest lands. There was to be only one kind of tree—conifer—just as there was only one class of dwellers in the countryside, workers, and one class of managers.

During the 1970s, East Germany suffered as badly as all the other European countries from the oil shortages and resulting large increase in price. A key factor in their production up until then was subsidized oil from the Soviet Union. That stopped abruptly. Apart from wood, the only other resource they had in sufficient quantity was brown lignite coal, the very worst type of fuel they could have used. In their haste, they resorted to open strip mining, destroying the land as they went. Lignite coal burns very messily, emitting heavy thick smoke with a lot of particulate matter. The public began complaining bitterly about pollution.

**Chapter 4: Reuniting Germany**

"Mr Gorbachev, tear down this wall." Ronald Reagan's words during a visit to Berlin resonated throughout the world in June

1987. It seemed an utterly improbable idea, but two years later the unimaginable happened and the wall was torn down. Seventy years of repression in the Soviet Union and forty years of repression in the satellite countries had not quenched the human desire to do things one's own way, worship if they chose, educate their children as they saw fit, and not live in a police state. The individual reasons for this desire were very disparate.

The socialist doctrine of atheism with its forced lack of religious observance motivated a great many older people. At least one very effective candlelight vigil was led by a Lutheran pastor in Dresden in 1988. For others, it was simply the capacity to say what one thought without ending up in jail. The chance to make more money and create a better future for the children was high on that list. Some were driven by a long-suppressed desire for better consumer goods, such as a nice car, reliable refrigerator, pretty clothes, and so forth. Once it became possible to watch Western television, the end approached rapidly. They could see how comfortably people just like themselves lived in the west, perhaps even their own relatives.

The specific events which oversaw the final destruction of Socialism/Communism as a governing principle and the reunification of Germany were very tumultuous. As will be shown by this book, the return to business autonomy or "freedom" was not a total success for many people. The reason in each case differed. Life can be very difficult for everyone, but for the East Germans, who had survived the almost total destruction of their country because of the Nazi regime and its Third Reich, and who were then taken over by a brutal dictatorship, it was even more difficult than for most. When they finally came out of all that darkness, they had almost no tools or resources to start over for a third time.

Hitler's regime only lasted twelve years, from 1933 to 1945, a microscopic period of time in world history—yet sufficient to wipe out Europe's Jews and cause catastrophic destruction all over the world, changing it forever. Whatever the East Germans' complicity in all these events was, they atoned mightily. There were many honorable men—florists, nursery owners and horticulturists—who served in Germany's forces under duress, but they too had to pay the price.

A few pieces of evidence support this assertion. Wilhelm Elsner, son and grandson of flower breeders in Dresden, was eighteen in 1940 and was obliged to join the German army. He had no more desire to kill anyone than fly to the moon, but he had no choice. Luckily for him, he was captured by the Americans fairly early in the war and spent most of the rest of the war in a prisoner of war camp in Oklahoma, far from any danger. When he recounted some of his experiences, he was able to draw the floor plan of the prison barracks in which he had lived.

The founder of the Ernst Benary seed firm had been Jewish but his children and descendants became Lutherans. In the family's tradition the eldest son took over the firm in each generation and at that epoch, it was Heinrich Benary. His eldest son, Heinz, was killed while fighting in the German army. Heinz's younger brother Friedrich moved the Benary Seed company to Hannover/Mund in West Germany.

**Handling freedom**

Once the rigid boundaries prescribing the flower breeders' every move were withdrawn, the vacuum which followed was totally unnerving. All the following may seem like a lot of needless detail but as they say, "The devil is in the details." It is one thing to make a large sweeping statement. It is another to prove it with layer upon layer of fact. This story confirms the hypothesis of this book. Remote planning not based on local reality or market forces was a failure.

A few small businesses were consolidated into cooperatives after reunification, and some of these actually succeeded. One of the first start-up companies was the GPG "Erfolg" (Success) in Marbach, near Erfurt. The GPG "Blumenstadt" (Flower City) developed into a notable cooperative known beyond the city limits for excellent perennials.

The formation of the GPG "Voran" (Go Forth) on April 1, 1960 in Erfurt had been a good omen for the future of Erfurt's horticulture. Five small nurseries and a flower shop decided to consolidate, and with this had a total of thirty hectares of farmland and some small greenhouses. The gardeners nominated Arthur Ruhe, an experienced master gardener previously with Heinemann, to be their chairman. Ruhe and members of the cooperative were very skillful and had a lot of foresight. The lone flower shop multiplied into more than twenty. Ruhe remained chairman up until his death thirty years later.

During the socialist era, Erfurt's administration had worked closely with these entities. Once the yearly planned requirement of vegetable production was reliably filled, it became possible to work on ornamental plants. Repeated use of the greenhouses worked out well. The planting of two hectares of carnations, one hectare of gerbera and large areas filled with hippeastrum, alstroemeria, and strelizia, enriched and diversified the cut flower offerings in the city of Erfurt.

A cooperative ended up having more freedom than any state-owned farm, and, back then, also had the freedom to choose its own investments and otherwise affect the financial outcome for its members. That was simply not possible for state-owned firms. The board of the cooperative, with strong leadership and motivated, well-trained employees guaranteed success for the company. After Arthur Ruhe died, Bernd Mueller took over and remained in charge until a few years after reunification.

With reunification, the company remained as a registered cooperative, didn't have a skilled worker shortage, and moved into the production of potted plants. Their main problem was supplying heat efficiently, the limited mechanization of the work processes, and the details of ownership of the land. The company is still functioning today, but with a different production structure. (JMT: this was written in 2014)

Very few former large cooperatives or state-owned farms survived the transition from the planned economy to the market economy. Some lasted for a short while, but only a small number of them made it in the long term. One sad example was in Henfstedt. To improve production, a two-hectare greenhouse complex was built. After reunification, the former head of this operation, Juergen Nietsche, bought it and still runs it today. He told Klaus Hoffmann that "Even now I am only working for the bank."

There were those who didn't succeed. One example of this is the former gardening cooperative in Bad Langensalza, GPG "Rote Oktober" (Red October). Only Volker Roenigk, part of the cooperative responsible for the tree nursery, was able to survive in a unified Germany.

The LPG in Grossburschla /Treffurt lost fifty percent of its land after reunification. The land went to three private horticultural companies, but only one is still in operation. The amount of planned produce was too large for local use but yet not large enough to be delivered to grocery chains. Selling their wares at weekly markets was not profitable. GPG Weimar was given back to the descendants of the former owner Welzel and was operated as a private corporation.

VE-Kombinat Muehlhausen was cobbled together from the horticultural enterprises of Arnstadt, Bleicherode, Ellrich, Geismar, and Muehlhausen. The company in Bleicherode was founded in 1926 and was one of the largest greenhouse complexes in Germany. The former directors of the state holding company, W. Bosem, W. Gajek and M. Herwig, were well-trained experts in horticulture and knew how to run a business. They claimed that no outside authority told them what they had to produce. That was possibly because everything they produced was in demand and without competition from other groups in the region. That fitted the category of "rarity."

VE-Kombinat Muehlhausen offered over three million cut roses, as well as laceleaf plants (*Filtonia*), different orchids, and foliage. They were able to sell these goods efficiently though their own flower shops in the region as well as with deliveries to the Cooperative Commercial Entities (KOV) in Erfurt, Halle,

Leipzig and Magdeburg. Despite initial attempts at privatization, nothing is left of this enormous state holding company.

After reunification, Erfurt tried to commercialize its products in the greater Thuringia area. Twenty-three businesses got together in 1992 to form the Breeders Collective (EZG) "Thueringer Zierpflanzen" (Thuringia's Ornamental Plants). It lasted for thirteen years, despite the fundamental problems which were ultimately existential: uneven and unstable production, delayed deliveries, and general unreliability of its members. The result was that the collective kept breaking down and eventually failed.

Another group, GPG "Georg Bock," grew chrysanthemums for cutting, using the large quantities of mother plants set out by the VEG in Mittelhausen. It seemed to work well but after 1989, all that remained of this cooperative was the tree nursery and the orchards.

Of these latter two operations, the tree nursery was returned to the family that previously owned it in 1990. Wilhelm and Thomas Kuehr are still working successfully today in Tiefthal as Kuehr's Tree and Rose Nursery. The orchards were taken over by Ernst Grossstueck and is still in business with a farm store between Marbach and Salomonsborn. (JMT: this was written in 2014)

Klaus Hoffmann wrote his book in order to honor those in horticulture who had to survive the punishing Socialist regime. The catastrophic condition of all Germany at the end of the war only made things worse for those who then had to knuckle under the Russians. Thuringia is a small state and horticulture was distributed across all of it. Its ornamental plant industry, once a leader in Germany, has shriveled to a small line of business.

## Chapter 5: Thuringia, the "green heart" of Germany and center of horticulture

Three states right in the center of Germany, Saxony, Thuringia, and Saxony-Anhalt, often called collectively "Middle Germany," were the hubs of floriculture. Within them, the cities of Erfurt and Quedlinburg had a tradition of agriculture and horticulture going back to medieval times. Later many more excellent nurseries developed. Two other regions were also very important and will be considered later. The land in and around Berlin was a center of flower production. A major botanical Garden, Berlin-Dahlem, reflects the historical involvement of that city. There was also a long history of great nurseries and brilliant plantsmen in Dresden, an historic city in East Germany.

## Erfurt: Blumenstadt or Flower City

Scholars say that the confluence of several large rivers mitigates the climate in Erfurt just enough to make it feasible to grow flowers successfully for commercial use, quite apart from maintaining a very reliable water supply. The bulwark of the Harz Mountains also shielded the plains from destructive winds. Rochester, New York, has a similar topography and was also known as a "Flower City" in the nineteenth century. An immigrant German gardening apprentice, Georg Ellwanger, took one look at the terrain when he was traveling around upstate New York by canal in the 1830s and immediately decided to settle there. Because he knew very little English he took on an Irishman, Patrick Barry, as a partner and together they developed one of the most successful businesses in the United States.

These favorable geographical conditions did not preclude remarkable nurseries and plantsmen being found throughout the rest of Germany: the Pfitzers in Fellbach and Kordes in Sparrieshoop come to mind. The difference was that they were spread out and did not have the same concentration of firms as there was in the major plant growing cities. Strong historical and economic factors also played a role in the rise of both cities.

Some of the successful nurseries in Erfurt and Quedlinburg had been founded a hundred and fifty or even two hundred years before this period, others were more recent. Hoffmann gives us useful sketches of these firms, a background to future events.

Originally Thuringia was very densely forested, sometimes termed "the green heart of Germany." Carving out agricultural land from forest required very hard work indeed but there were solid reasons for the impressive development of Erfurt and its surrounding area as a rich agricultural and horticultural region.

One was the nature of the soil and a reliable water supply from the Saale River. Another was that Christianity established itself in this area earlier than other parts of Middle Germany. Large monasteries in Thuringia brought stability, patronage, and employment for many serfs. One of the earliest monasteries dates back to 1216. The Augustinian Monastery of Erfurt was built in the thirteenth century.

The resulting growth of the population made it necessary to find food for everyone. The increased population and thus trade were very beneficial for this small town. Augustinian monks were cosmopolitan educated men. They started schools and even a university, an amenity which the citizens had never had before. The money to build it came from Erfurt's woad traders. (see below) The university was founded in 1379 and is one of the oldest such schools in Germany. One well-known graduate was Martin Luther.

The presence of the monasteries and churches, many of which still exist today, led to an early nickname, "Rome of the North." The Cathedral, the Church of St Severus, and the All Holy Church are very impressive. Much of the land belonged to the Church and the various foundations benefited from the income.

**Christian Reichart: A founding figure of horticulture in Erfurt**

Hoffmann considered, not without reason, that the birth of Christian Reichart on July 4, 1685, was the foundation of scientific horticulture in Erfurt. Reichart's father came from a wealthy Erfurt family. Hoffmann waxed lyrical over Reichart's birth, calling Erfurt "the cradle of horticulture." Reichart lived to be ninety years old.

His birth year, 1685, was very auspicious. Johann Sebastian Bach, Georg Frideric Handel, and Antonio Vivaldi were all born that year.

Christian Reichart, 1685 – 1775, Founder of Erfurt
horticulture Reproduced by permission: Klaus Hoffmann

Unfortunately, Reichart's father died when Christian was very young, but his mother married another very fine man, Christoph Engelhardt, who treated the boy as his own. Engelhardt set Christian an example in his own life and actively guided the child's education and career. The story of Amadeo Giannini, founder of the Bank of America, was very similar, with the murder of his father when he was seven years old and his mother's remarriage. His stepfather too formed Giannini's character. It is possible for love to conquer all.

Christian Reichart studied Law at the University of Erfurt as well as at other colleges. After graduation Reichart held numerous jobs, including a stint as a councilor in the Erfurt City Hall with varied and wide-ranging responsibilities. He thought deeply about the work in front of him, but his mind also ranged into many other realms. He was responsible for city planning and development and architectural design in the city, but more abstract questions of citizens' rights and fire protection concerned him too. In the background were questions about agriculture and horticulture. Eventually, that was where he made his greatest contribution because of his love and respect for his stepfather.

The period in which Reichart was active was relatively free of serious wars. That allowed space for much intellectual growth throughout Europe and the precursor of modern Germany.

Germany was still a series of loosely connected principalities under the rule of the holy Roman Emperor. Technically, Erfurt was under the control of the Electorate of Mainz, which built a large fortress there in 1690. This did not seem to be a problem for the citizens as they went about their business.

When his stepfather, Christoph Engelhardt, became ill in 1720, Reichart devoted himself to his care for two years. Englehardt was the best and most successful farmer in the city. During this illness, which lasted until 1722, he was not able to continue managing his land. Reichart did it for him.

Engelhardt had taught himself farming but he was most interested in plants. We are fortunate that he diligently kept a journal with a surprisingly large number of technical suggestions and detailed information. After his stepfather's death, Christian Reichart focused exclusively on farming. He and his mother had inherited all Engelhardt's property. He too kept copious notes. His property was in what is now called the "Dreienbrunnengebiet" (Three-Well-Area, in south Erfurt).

Reichart began by experimenting with watercress. Salads were not a serious article of diet in the early 18th century the way they are now, but the constantly flowing, temperate water coming from the mountains made for perfect watercress beds. In the wild, the cress grows along the banks of gentle streams and rivers. It does not grow in standing water. On Reichart's property, it grew very well all year round. He created a sophisticated production process in the beds of water and left detailed notes about it in his journal.

Watercress was one of the first plants grown on a big enough scale to be widely marketed, and it made Erfurt famous well beyond its borders. Napoleon was said to have taken his court gardener with him to Erfurt in order to see these plants and learn how to grow them. He thought he could develop something similar in France. In the end he took two experienced gardeners back with him to France: Nottrodt, from Erfurt, and Zugwurst from Vieselbach.

This story seems a bit fishy to us now. Watercress had been grown in the French department of Picardy since the 15th century. (JMT note: Napoleon's visit may be a myth but the two gardeners did leave Erfurt. No written reference to the Napoleon visit has been found.)

Cauliflower was Reichart's next project. He wanted to improve the cultivation of vegetables. At the time, the only cauliflower seeds came from Cyprus. Somehow, Reichart managed to produce his own cauliflower seeds. This was a good choice. Cauliflower is more expensive than other vegetables and thus a good source of income.

Reichart then turned his attention to flower seeds. He made modifications which led to the flow of seeds becoming more predictable and dependable. That too increased profitability. In all, Reichart developed 93 different types of vegetable and flower varieties. All his moves were very lucrative. Other farmers quickly copied him.

Reichart developed technical devices to reduce some of the heavier work in the fields and described them in his notes. One was a spiked roller to loosen hard soil. He really wanted to be sure his ideas and solutions were passed on to future generations. This desire culminated in a six-volume work: *The Treasure of Land and Garden.* The first volume came out in 1752.

In those years there were very few textbooks of agriculture and horticulture. One or two were written in the fifteenth century. Educated farmers who could read often still referred to Roman texts from the first two centuries of the Common Era. In the main, practical farming knowledge passed to the next generation from father to son. The idea that farming could somehow be learned from a book was still far off.

Reichart's books can be very illuminating reading for horticulture apprentices. They cover plant breeding and cultivation with the focus on seeds, vegetable production, and crop rotation. Reichart showed it was not necessary to leave the land fallow for long periods of time if one planted complementary crops instead. He also included information about growing hops, very important in a place with so many breweries.

Reichart was a very special citizen of Erfurt. Even at that time he was well known far beyond Erfurt. The city fathers erected a large monument in honor of him. On an especially beautiful pedestal, one can see an "upstanding" and powerful citizen, the creator of Thuringian horticulture.

Horticulture developed serially, depending on the needs of the community. In addition to basic staples Erfurt saw viticulture, pomiculture, and woad production in that order, followed by watercress development and then vegetables and flowers.

All these crops remain important in Thuringia except viticulture and woad (*Isatis tinctoria*). The woad trade collapsed first with competition from the superior vegetable dye indigo eluted from *Indigofera tinctoria* and then later with the discovery of synthetic aniline dyes, ironically in Germany. The weavers of Nimes in France used indigo in the mid-nineteenth century to dye their cotton cloth denim: hence "blue jeans."

The end of the woad industry freed up a good deal of excellent arable land in the Thuringia basin that could then be used for ornamental plants. A new source of gold was found. As the demand for Erfurt wine fell off and the farmers ceased tending their vines, this land also became available for other crops.

One of the most important crops was sugar beet. It may not be glamorous or beautiful, but it was indispensable and built a number of fortunes in Thuringia. Sugar beet was also the mainstay in Quedlinburg in the neighboring state of Saxony-Anhalt. The fertile soil combined with the ideal climate also offered excellent conditions for other vegetables and the cultivation of flowers there.

Flowers were mainly grown for their seed. That was where money could be made, both in Germany and abroad, starting in the late eighteenth century. At a time when communications were still completely primitive it was not possible to send plants for any distance, but seed was far more resistant to long delays and careless handling. There had always been notable exceptions. Queen Hatshepshut of Egypt got her frankincense trees well wrapped up directly from the Land of Punt. The murals in her tomb show the trees arriving.

Reichart may have developed the foundation and offered a vision for a new horticulture, but the next step was to improve the mechanics of the market. This became possible with the seed trade. There were no hidebound rules to prevent it.

## Individual firms

Reichart showed the way and after his death other men began growing plants for seed. To form an idea of what things were like in Erfurt in the late 1930s, before the war, it is necessary to go back into the Erfurt of more than two hundred years ago. Jakob Platz started a nursery in 1756 and Franz Anton Haage in 1778. They were followed by Friedrich Adolph Haage in 1822 and Johan C. Schmidt in1823. Ernst Benary came a bit later, in1843. Franz Carl Heinemann (1848), Haage & Schmidt and Niels Lund Chrestensen opened for business in 1867 and Carl Weigelt in 1895.

## Jakob Platz

Jakob Platz set up one of the first commercial nurseries in Erfurt. The firm produced a large range of different sorts of seeds for sale. Platz printed its first seed catalog in 1788 and distributed it to many other towns and cities. This was quite innovative at the time. Sending mail was not the straightforward and simple process we have now. It involved a lot of hard riding along pretty bad roads, with the price lists entrusted to carters who slowly made their way from town to town. The Platz nursery continued in business for a long time.

So far, that catalogue has not been found. Someone named Carl Platz owned a nursery in Erfurt in the early 1830s and issued a number of catalogues. One or two of these were saved. Possibly he was related to Jakob.

**The Haage family**

The Haage family's name appears in the city chronicles and archives generation after generation as they were quite central to its history and growth. Ilsabe Schalldach contributed a piece about this dynasty in "Blumenstadt Erfurt," a compilation of the history of Erfurt's nursery industry.

The house in Dreienbrunnenfeld where Johann Heinrich Haage ran his gardening center, starting on October 25, 1769, is marked with a plaque. One of his sons and many of his descendants also went into horticulture. The family firm lasted until 1960. If the Russians had not taken over East Germany, it might still be in business today. Just as a footnote, Haage sold watercress in addition to other salad greens.

In 1960, his descendant Fritz Haage refused to join the new GPG, the Horticultural Production Cooperative. Such disobedience was punished very brutally. He lost everything. The watercress beds went to ruin. An attempt to grow watercress again in the 1980s was unsuccessful.

Once Germany was reunited, Fritz Haage's son, who had fled to West Germany, received his land back but then sold it all to a local man named Emil Liedke. Liedke created a park-like garden on it and added a trout farm later.

Other branches of this significant horticultural family were able to hold on to their nurseries. Johann Heinrich Haage's (1737-1800) grandson was Friedrich Adolph Haage, 1796-1866. This man was apprenticed to the court gardener in Dresden, Johann Heinrich Seidel. The Seidels were also a large gardening clan and one or two of them were every important in the development of the camellia in Europe.

Friedrich Adolph was very conscientious and received a commendation during his apprenticeship. His prize was a cactus seedling, 'King of the Night,' a night-blooming cereus. Their flowers have an almost mystical appeal. This could have been the inspiration for the future Kakteen Haage, the Haage Cactus Garden Center.

Haage's nursery became the leading center in Germany for cacti and other succulents. His grandson, Walter Haage (1899-1992), was a famous expert and author of influential text books about cacti, more of a scholar than a businessman. Tours through this cactus collection, which Klaus Hoffmann had enjoyed, were said to be truly a remarkable experience.

In 1972 the company was nationalized. Walter's son Hans-Friedrich, another excellent professional and a graduate of Humboldt University, was the head of the company, and his father remained in charge of breeding for some time. This was all to the good.

Two years later, the nationalized company became associated with the VEG Seed Production of Ornamental Plants in Erfurt. Considering the situation at the time, this was a positive move for a company which had lagged badly. The government allowed Haage to build new greenhouses, but these were too large for cacti alone. Even when the demand for cacti was very high in the 1970s, they could not fill the entire space with cacti and had to take on other kinds of plant for export. Hans Friedrich Haage was appointed to be head of the state Commodity Subgroup Cacti. That was a good choice. Under his direction, the cactus crops earned valuable income in the DDR.

There is a story from another source that Haage was also allowed to have extra supplies of fuel for the greenhouses during the punishingly cold winter of 1947. One of the socialist officials was a botanist with a serious interest in exotic plants. That person later became the director of the Moscow Botanical Garden and looked out for the firm.

With reunification, the company was restored to its original owners. The next generation completely changed direction. The nursery became a "Destination Garden Center for Cacti," where people could enjoy the plants but also buy unusual specimens. Ulrich Haage is the owner today. Hoffmann wrote that Haage was also president of the state association for horticulture in Thuringia in 2010, a voluntary position.

Johann Nicolaus Haage (1739-1787), Johann Heinrich Haage's brother, was one of the founders of Haage and Schmidt, a famous firm which lasted from the early nineteenth century until the end of WWII. At that point it was liquidated. A training center for horticulture was built on part of its land, making use of some of its buildings.

The company belonging to Franz Anton Haage (1763-1836) and his descendants also played an important role in Erfurt's horticulture. With this extraordinary history of a single family, one wonders why the city was not renamed "Haagestadt."

**Johann Christoph Schmidt**

In 1829 Johann Christoph Schmidt, 1753 – 1829, opened a totally new kind of nursery and garden store. He operated out of a former soap and wax factory and offered a much wider range of merchandise than had hitherto been sold all in one place. In its own way it was a prototype of a modern garden center.

He sold fresh flowers, potted plants, dried flowers, bouquets, and a wide variety of flower seeds, particularly dahlia seeds, as well as all sorts of ties and ribbons for making bouquets. This was a very novel concept at a time when well-born ladies would seldom deign even to enter a shop, but made the shopkeeper come to her with his wares.

Schmidt also had a nursery for fruit trees, berries, and rose bushes. Many years later they started to use a large tract of open land near their premises for their own breeding experiments. Old catalogs show the large variety of different articles available for sale. There are still remnants of J. C. Schmidt's warehouses and greenhouses in Erfurt giving some idea of the extent of this company. (JMT: written in 2011)

Klaus Hoffmann took over the management of the Leipzig Street branch of the VEG Seed Production of Ornamental Plants soon after graduating from Humboldt University. There he learned about parts of J.C. Schmidt's former company, worked on the cold frame facilities, struggled with the old heating system and could reflect on what it must have been like during the "glory days."

Schmidt's had begun to decline during the First World War, and by the late 1920s was rapidly going downhill. Ernst Benary's firm did its best to prevent Schmidt's bankruptcy. Wilhelm Benary took over J. C. Schmidt's in 1929. By transforming it into a new LLC, he led the company quite profitably up until its nationalization.

## Ernst Benary

Ernst Benary, 1819 – 1893, started one of the most important nurseries in Erfurt. He began modestly enough, primarily growing and selling vegetable seeds. That was common in those days. What was not so usual was that Benary was a Jew. Almost no Jews ever went into horticulture, as they had never been allowed to own land.

Ernst Benary, 1819 – 1893, founder of the Benary seed firm
in Erfurt   Reproduced by permission: Klaus Hoffmann

His family had been bankers and quite wealthy but the fortune evaporated when the Elector touched his father for a "loan." Ernst was the eighth child in a family of nine and the youngest son. His father had died and his elder brothers could not afford to do much for him. They apprenticed him to the well-known nursery of Haage & Schmidt because he was fond of nature and the outdoors. The surprising thing was that Haage & Schmidt accepted him. This was a few years after Napoleon had emancipated Europe's Jews and perhaps Herr Haage had more modern views.

Flowers were not quite so central for the public at the time but with the end of the Napoleonic Wars and a slow increase in middle class prosperity, it became possible for a person of relatively modest means to buy a house with a small plot of land around it and thus the desire to create a garden. That is when flower seeds entered into their own.

A fairly short time after opening his business, Benary rented land and created his own garden center. This expansion prospered very quickly under his leadership, with Benary becoming an important company. He and his wife worked very hard in those early days, sitting up late at night to weigh out seed to send to customers.

There is tantalizingly suggestive evidence that Benary sold green and yellow pea seeds to the Abbé Gregor Mendel at the Augustinian Monastery of St Thomas in Brno and perhaps some other types of peas too. Mendel laid the foundation of modern genetics by showing how the ratios of green and yellow plants followed clear patterns after the first and second crossings. A few Benary invoices for flower seeds in the 1870s have turned up in the monastery's archives, but the other monks burned every scrap of paper relating to Mendel's work after his death. There is nothing concrete.

Benary recognized the value in offering many different kinds of related goods quite early, just as Johann Christoph Schmidt had done about twenty years earlier. For this he needed motivated, talented, and well-trained employees who could work independently and could implement ideas and plans accurately and dependably. Ernst Benary expected a lot from his employees, but also kept his end of the implicit bargain. He made sure they had good housing, places for recreation, and a sick fund in the event of illness. Well-treated workers are far more productive than badly treated ones. Like many successful businessmen, Benary also played a significant role in city government. This was beneficial both to the city and to the business. He initiated a number of the attractions that later brought both tourists and horticultural specialists to the city.

The firm reached the pinnacle of social recognition when the Kaiserin Victoria, Queen Victoria's daughter, visited Benary's one afternoon. Frau Benary was very quick-thinking. Realizing that the Kaiserin would be hot and thirsty after traveling for a long time, she invited her into her own home and turned the living room over to the queen and her entourage. This was much appreciated.

All Benary's children converted to Christianity and became Lutherans. After Ernst died, his sons Friedrich and John took over. They too had excellent management skills. Friedrich and John had studied languages and used this to expand beyond the German borders. They issued catalogues both in English and French. By dividing the responsibilities appropriately and setting strategic goals, they succeeded in increasing flower and vegetable seed production quite noticeably. They also continued their father's concern for their workers.

Until the outbreak of World War I, the company utilized thirty-five hectares of land and had fifteen hectares of glass and rack facilities. The racks held seed packages. Two hundred and fifty workers were kept busy all year around. World War I brought large cuts and unpleasant consequences for Benary's. Profits fell, partly because they had lost many customers and also their skilled workers. The situation improved in the 1930s by the time Ernst Benary's grandsons, Ernst and Heinrich, took over. Alas, this recovery was short lived.

The rise of the Nazis threatened the family because of their Jewish origins and led to difficulties with the management of the company. According to members of the family, some of their employees stood by them heroically throughout this very dangerous period. The war itself also affected the family very badly. Heinrich's only son Heinz fought with the German army and was killed in action during World War II. The glass in their greenhouses was blown out by Allied bombing. The Nazi government made clear to them that if they used all their land to produce food for the German forces and stopped growing flowers they might just, and only just, be allowed to continue in business, and the Jewish ancestors might be temporarily overlooked. The Benarys had no choice.

Even though the Benary children had all become Lutheran by the second generation, their very name is a version of the Hebrew "Ben Ari," son of Ari. The Nazis never lost sight of that. The Benary's necessary extra vigilance made the family particularly sensitive to the looming threat after the end of the war. More than anyone else, they saw trouble ahead with the departure of the Americans from their sector and the arrival of the Russians. The elder Benarys wasted no time but sent another of Ernst's descendants, Friedrich, west to Hannover/Mund in 1946 to start over even before their persecution by the Russians began.

Once the war ended, the Benary family slowly resumed their previous work. It took them a very long time to replace the glass in their greenhouses, which had been knocked out by Allied bombing. While they were doing that, they watched the Russians coming closer and closer with increasing dread.

While it was still possible to leave East Germany, Friedrich Benary moved by himself to Hannover-Munden in West Germany in 1946. He could not take very much money with him, but after a lot of effort he started a new nursery. Friedrich Benary issued the first catalogue of his new business in 1949, a single page of mimeographed typescript. The following year he was able to produce a proper printed catalogue.

It did not take long for the new occupiers to trump up false charges against them. By 1951 the Socialist government accused Benary of tax evasion *in absentia* and threatened them with imprisonment. The bogus accusations and possibility of a show trial had propelled the rest of the family into all leaving the DDR two years before. In doing so, they abandoned everything they had: the business, land, houses, and all other property.

Once in West Germany, some former employees helped them rebuild. This successor, the Benary Seed Company, is known nationally and internationally for its important contributions to horticulture.

The Benary Company of Erfurt ceased to exist in Erfurt by 1952 after having been around for over 100 years. In recognition of the firm's huge contributions to the town's prosperity, Erfurt somewhat belatedly erected a monument to Ernst Benary in 2000. Following reunification, the Benarys tried to regain their property but were rejected. They took the case to the German high court but the court ruled against them. The property had long ago been given to one of their rivals and this firm maintained its claim. The rivals invested heavily in the place and have done very well in Erfurt. Benary Company has remained in Hannover-Munden ever since.

The West German division of Benary grew and expanded while the East German relic withered. Benary is now a global firm with branches in the United States and other countries. The present owner is a sixth-generation descendant of great-great-great-grandpa Ernst, Klaudia.


**N.L Chrestensen**

(adapted from an article by Wolf-Dieter Blüthner in "Blumenstadt Erfurt")

The founder of this nursery in Erfurt, Niels Lund Chrestensen, the eldest son of a Danish farming family, was born in 1840. After his training and apprenticeship with an Aarhus nursery, he decided to seek better opportunities abroad. There was very little for him in Denmark.

He was drawn to Erfurt, whose fine reputation for horticulture was well known in Denmark. There had been a large flower and garden show in Erfurt in 1840, which was followed by a number of other important horticultural events that established the city as a horticultural center. Niels arrived in Erfurt in 1862 and found work first at the Schierlitz & Moschkowitz nursery and later at the Gebrueder Born nursery, which produced vinegars and mustard in addition to plants and seeds.

Due to strained political relations between Germany and Denmark, Niels decided not to return to his home country and to stay in Erfurt where he wanted to set up a business of his own. When he was awarded citizenship, he noticed that his surname "Christensen" had been misspelled as "Chrestensen." He kept it that way from then on. His talent for flower arranging was evident at the flower and garden show in Erfurt in 1865 and was particularly admired.

He established his own small business in 1867, located in the center of the town at Marktstrasse 14. Later, he moved down the street and opened a florist shop specializing in locally grown grasses, ferns, everlasting (*Xeranthemum*), ornamental shrubs, and cut flowers, which he made into striking bouquets and wreaths.

Chrestensen devised methods for keeping the plants fresh and others for dyeing the grasses and ferns. Thanks to his artistic talent and good business sense, he was very successful and became well-known. He married Auguste Kujawa in 1870, and in a few years had saved enough money to buy a handsome old building which is still in family hands. Their son Carl was born in 1876.

When the Prussian government ordered the dismantling of Erfurt's ancient city walls in 1873, these nursery firms suddenly had access to a large amount of additional land. That enabled some of them to expand very considerably. Ten years later the floricultural firms in Erfurt got together and formed a trade association.

A highlight in Niels Lund's career was arranging the flowers for the German crown prince's silver wedding anniversary in January of 1883. Following that, Chrestensen was named court florist to the Kaiser, and later also to the Austro-Hungarian monarchs. He posted the coats of arms at the entrance to his business, announcing his connection to these special customers.

Chrestensen took advantage of new technology very quickly. Erfurt's first telephone link was not from the city hall to council members, but from Chrestensen's business at Markstrasse 38 to his nursery in the Aue. It was three years before the Reich post office set up a telephone line.

In addition to his work in Erfurt, Chrestensen took part in many national and international horticultural expositions. He participated in the renowned world expo in Chicago in 1893. There he presented 'Viola tricolor' and received the Columbus Medal. This trip to Chicago may have been some consolation for the loss of his wife, who had died after a long battle with cancer in 1892.

Three years later, Niels married Adele Ludwig, the daughter of an Elberfeld brewer. With her good business and book keeping skills, Adele became an important asset to the Chrestensen enterprise. She had one son, Willie.

While in St. Petersburg, Chrestensen met a Berlin horticulturist, Herr Huebner, who had a small chain of florist shops around the turn of the century. Together, they came up with the idea of organizing a way of placing orders by telephone or telegram. Their collaboration on this later became what is internationally known as Fleurop, an international florist's delivery service.

After this big international flower show in St. Petersburg in 1899, Niels kept closer to home due to his second wife's illness. In order to serve his British customers better, he established a London branch in 1899, which was run by his elder son, Carl, and then later by a man by the name of Mills.

Around the turn of the 20th century, the N.L. Chrestensen firm employed 160 workers full time. In addition, a large number of temporary workers tended the fields of lily of the valley. Chrestensen was the largest exporter of these seeds in the world. Beside grasses and seeds, the nursery offered grains, potatoes, and rhubarb.

He created a book called *Chrestensen's illustriertes Handbuch fuer Feld und Gartenbau* (Illustrated Guidebook for Field and Garden Plants) to document his experience and knowledge for his customers. By 1917, there were thirty-five varieties of vegetables and other crop plants in his catalogue. He used his own crops as well as some from other German nurseries and abroad.

In spite of having left Denmark forty years earlier, he was very proud of receiving the Danneborg Orden in 1906, an honor which was normally reserved for Danish residents. Aside from all the attention he paid to his business, Niels was also an active member of Erfurt society. He had close ties with the University of Berlin and University of St. Petersburg. Chrestensen had the same philosophy about his workers as his peers in Erfurt. He treated his large staff very well.

Group of notable Erfurt nurserymen   Reproduced
by permission: Klaus Hoffmann

Niels Lund Chrestensen died on January 21, 1914, leaving behind a flourishing business run by his second wife, Adele. She was very competent as a bookkeeper, but had difficulty managing the male-dominated business. Entrenched senior managers were not accustomed to being told what to do by a woman. She turned to her son Willie to help her.

The outbreak of WW I in 1914, led to hard times in Erfurt. The Chrestensen nursery, along with others, increased vegetable production in order to help with the food supply, but conditions remained catastrophic. The loss of 3,579 soldiers and countless wounded from Thuringia was a big blow, as well as the large number of those who died of hunger and illness. Willie Chrestensen was killed in the last days of the war, leaving his half-brother Carl as his successor. Carl Chrestensen then became manager of the Erfurt headquarters after his stepmother Adele's death in 1919. Towards the end of 1920 the company acquired its first motor vehicles: a used car and a truck with rubber tires.

After the fall of the German monarchy in 1918, the Chrestensens wisely removed the royal coats of arms from their property. Rather unexpectedly, so many society events required glittering floral decorations in the 1920s that Carl Chrestensen came close to abandoning the horticultural aspect of the business and focusing on parties only. This made it difficult for his son, Niels, and the manager, Thiel, to restore the original plant and seed business in the early 1930s. In 1925, Carl had expanded his responsibilities to include sales and involvement in seed production. An office in London was an important part of this. He continued to spend six months each year in England, running the London end of the business.

Postwar inflation created a very challenging environment for many formerly successful businesses. What did hold value was real estate and a solid inventory of useful products. Memories of wartime brutality led many foreign customers to boycott German goods, resulting in the collapse of many German businesses. In spite of such difficulties, N.L. Chrestensen was able to stay afloat and even expand its horticultural market share. The business of providing decorations for cotillions continued to do well, especially with the use of a new product, raffia, imported from Madagascar. It was dyed in thirty-one different colors and was very popular for crafts and all sorts of decorations.

When Hitler took over the government on January 30, 1933, Carl Chrestensen was convinced that this did not bode well. He was right. Once World War Two was underway, the firm was required to start cultivating food supplies for the nation. The Nazi government body in charge of this, the Reichsnaehrstand, took over an existing organization of various horticultural and agricultural businesses and forced them to comply with the new rules.

The Reichsnaehrstand determined which crops should be grown and how much of them. For example, Chrestensen was ordered to produce thirty tons of cauliflower (shades of Reichart and his experiments with cauliflower). How this could be done was left to the producer to decide. In spite of the overwhelming demands, Chrestensen still managed to develop new vegetables. All this left very little time or space for breeding flowers, but they did come up with one new variety of aster, Chrestensen's 'Komet Aster Express.'

Carl's son, Niels, was born in 1907. In 1929, Niels went to London to work in that branch of the business part of the year. He returned to Erfurt for good in 1937 when the Nazis ordered everyone to cease doing business abroad. Niels was drafted into the service in 1939, rather a ripe age for a soldier, and served as a guard in Teplitz-Schoenau. His father's death just a couple of months later allowed his mother to get him released from the army. Niels returned to Erfurt to manage the business, the third generation of Chrestensens.

Exactly what impact the war years had on the output and production of the nursery businesses cannot be measured. Catalogues during this time show that horticultural production continued, in spite of the fact that all aspects of commerce and industry were affected by the war. The government tried to offset the reduced workforce because of workers being drafted or enlisting by bringing in guest workers or forced labor. Five hundred Italian workers, for instance, were brought in to work in the various Erfurt nurseries. Young volunteers came to help out at Chrestensens in the spring of 1941. Chrestensen says they never used forced labor.

Niels' two sons, Niels Lund and Cornel, worked together to run the family business. By the time of the company's nationalization in February of 1972 Niels Lund had been a leading member of the DDR's seed and plant cultivation overseeing 9,000 hectares of crops from the planning stages to harvest. Between 1972 and 1990 he was a delegate to Erfurt's city council, where he served as chair of a horticultural committee. He was very involved in the National Democratic Party and was recognized by the government for his contributions to the Fatherland, receiving a number of silver medals.

What had been the N.L. Chrestensen firm was folded into the VEB (state-owned business) Erfurt Flower Seeds. Cornel worked there as head of the sales department and his wife worked in exports. Niels Lund was the head of seed and plant cultivation, while his wife managed the nursery and florist business in the Marktstrasse.

The focus of the VEB Erfurt for ornamental plants was seed production, a matter that Niels Lund and the managing director agreed upon, though questions about how this was to be achieved led to frequent arguments. They were also concerned about the working conditions of the employees. The authorities allowed them to build a new "social building" to much acclaim. Unfortunately, it was assigned to the VEG Seed Production, thus being a "lost" investment by the VEB. The latter workers were unable to enjoy its amenities. During the DDR years, talent for improvisation and a wealth of ideas had to compensate for lack of attention to capital investment needs.

Between 1972 and 1990, the VEB introduced eleven new vegetables, three new medicinal and herbal plants, and 161 new ornamental plants. Because of the collective aspect of the nursery business during those years, Chrestensen-bred plants were not clearly identified.

In 1973, the management of the collectives decided to start a nursery mail-order business based in Erfurt, designed to compete with similar businesses in West Germany and to be a forerunner of future operations in the DDR. Party leaders knew of N.L. Chrestensen's former flourishing mail-order business, and they meant to take advantage of the expertise of its employees. Cornel Chrestensen was named director of the mail-order business.

By 1987, the VEB Erfurt Flower Seeds had far and away more shipments than any of the others. They shipped an aggregate of 425,000 orders, more than 1,100 per day. This enormous workload was handled by 208 employees and all within only a few weeks since private gardeners start getting ready for the season and placing their orders in the spring. Orders from 135,900 customers brought in over four million marks.

The DDR leaders were particularly interested in developing good business relations with the neighboring socialist countries, but trade with Western countries was even more desirable, since it brought in foreign exchange. N.L. Chrestensen remained private up until 1959 and could plan its own business dealings for the most part. It still had to comply with requirements of the central planning commission however. Any profit they made went mostly to the state. N.L. Chrestensen paid taxes of 93%.

This semi-independence changed once the firm was nationalized (expropriated). New rules were set in place in 1972. Any former contracts for foreign trade with N.L. Chrestensen were canceled and all Chrestensen's foreign customers and files were turned over to the VEB Seed and Plants of Erfurt.

In spite of this, contacts with other socialist countries were important to the VEB Erfurt Seeds for Ornamental Plants. This was not only due to the economic advantages the contacts offered, but also to the personal interest both Chrestensens had in this aspect of the business. Cornel Chrestensen had secured a long-term contract for seed shipments to the Soviet Union while he was in Kiev for a semester. As the director of mail order, Cornel made many trips to Bulgaria, Rumania and Czechoslovakia.

Everyone worked as hard as they could within the constraints imposed by the VEB system, including the Chrestensen family itself. They tried their best to adapt to the changes, but economic and political reality nullified all this. Just a few months after the new rulings on re-privatization in March of 1990, the

Chrestensen family applied to get their land and family business back. The former managers began to think about the future of the Erfurt Flower Seed VEB.

While this was going on, Cornel discovered someone in management had collected all the addresses of the VEB customers and was preparing to sell them to a West German mail-order company. That individual was dismissed and disappeared the very same day. He was never heard from again. Dropped down into an oubliette perhaps?

On June 25, 1990, the Chrestensen firm finally regained its independence and was restructured into a GmbH. This was one of the happiest days in Niels Lund's life. He had brought the old family-owned business full circle. Sadly, he died on December 2, 1990, just six months after the privatization.

At this time, Chrestensens had seven different production locations in Erfurt and more sales offices outside the town, operated by seven hundred employees. The company assets amounted only to about 9,000 DMarks. An Erfurt bank issued them credit for operating expenses the following year based only on a handwritten estimate of costs and income.

All the business contacts that had been managed by the VEG's central administrative office had to be revived and old customers brought back on board. Many structural improvements were needed to modernize the facilities. They invested heavily in storage space, greenhouses and a new garden center as well as modern computers. They intensified their breeding of new plants, resulting in seven new vegetable varieties, five new herbs and medicinal plants, and 122 new ornamental plants.

A new era began for the company in 2007 when Frederick Niels Chrestensen became general manager. Now, twenty years after reunification, the company remains successful, with many different branches and sales offices. Much of the seed cultivation is now farmed out to other countries in Europe, Africa, and Asia. Sales are once again international, but there is still a large local garden center with seeds, plants, containers and other relevant merchandise. They have 120 full-time employees and a large number of seasonal workers, plus twenty-five or thirty apprentices. The company treats its women employees well by paying them properly and giving them some flexibility in their hours, and has received many awards for outstanding business practices.

**F.C. Heinemann**

(based on an article by Eberhard Czekalla in "Blumenstadt Erfurt")

The F.C. Heinemann Company was one of the biggest seed companies in Erfurt during the 19th and 20th centuries. Very little has been written about it since the nationalization of 1972, but some information came from Ruth and Eberhard Menzel, Juergen Valdeig, and Steffen Rassloff. Eberhard Czekalla himself was employed by the company from 1961 – 1968, and examines the history of the company in this chapter as well as the political implications of the times.

Franz Carl Heinemann founded it in the tumultuous period of 1848. His family came from Eichsfeld in Thuringia. His father, Karl Wilhelm Anton Heinemann, was a district magistrate serving on the Grand Duke of Weimar's Royal Council and as such could afford a very good education for his son, Franz Carl Heinemann. Karl worked for twenty-five years in Vieselbach and was highly regarded.

His son Franz was born there on March 10, 1833. He was graduated from the Erfurt Gymnasium, where he had made friends with Ernst Benary in the same class. Benary later became an apprentice at Haage & Schmidt. Apparently Heinemann was intrigued by this, and he too decided to continue with vocational training as a gardener. Here was another curious situation: the son of a magistrate getting his hands dirty as a gardener. Heinemann worked at the Royal Belvedere gardens near Weimar before going on to study natural science in Jena in 1839. Later, he worked in the nursery field in Potsdam, France, England, and Belgium (Ghent), and was the director of the Rosenthal tree nursery in Vienna.

He founded his own firm on April 1, 1848 in Erfurt. He had already started growing plants on a plot of land around the "Kohlgrube." In 1850, he added another piece of land in the Weidengasse, where he built the company's warehouses, barns, and main office. Heinemann's father gave him seven thousand marks to get started. He used it to purchase seeds and plants. His capable wife Irene assisted him and he was soon able to cultivate his own stock, especially summer flowers, biennials, potted plants, and vegetables.

In a very short time he began to offer 141 types of vegetables and 383 sorts of flowers for sale. He had aimed right from the start for this this wonderful choice of seeds and plants, knowing it would catch the public's eye. He imported bulbs from Holland and sold roses, fuchsia, verbena, chrysanthemums, dahlia, palms, and other hothouse plants and rhododendron. (As an aside, that was early for rhododendron. Some of the great discoveries in the Himalayas had not yet been made.) A few years later Heinemann listed 2,600 plants, and by 1857 there were 4,000. There were two hundred varieties of roses alone. In addition, he offered fruit trees and grape vines.

F. C. Heinemann was very deft at advertising. He adopted the practice of adding pictures, and later color, to his price lists very early. This was expensive, but the return justified it. It is possible he had learned how to present such an abundance of flowers from the example of Louis van Houtte in Belgium, a slightly larger-than-life figure in the history of European horticulture.

At first, Heinemann issued his main catalogue in the autumn, but after 1861 he switched to showing what was available in the spring. His list of cactus included 800 different varieties. Heinemann printed an even more gorgeous colored edition of his nursery stock for the Erfurt flower show in 1865. His company was honored at this show by the Kaiserin.

Heinemann had lots of contacts in the field, not only in Germany, but all over the world. Some were named in the company "Festschrift." It listed growers and horticulturists from the USA, France, England, Belgium, Brazil, Russia, Switzerland, and Japan.

They distributed the catalogues widely in Austria, with prices in Austrian currency. Starting in 1874, catalogues for the English and French markets were printed in those languages and were distributed up until WW I. After F. C. Heinemann's death on October 28, 1875 at the age of 56, his widow and their three sons took over the company. It is not surprising that he died relatively young with such strenuous achievements behind him.

The eldest son, Friedrich Carl, was born in 1850. His brother Kurt was born in in 1852 and his youngest brother Franz in 1860. All three brothers contributed to the business but Kurt died young at the age of thirty-three. Friedrich expanded the company's base and continued publishing attractive catalogues as well as maintaining a horticultural library for interested customers. The third son, Franz, devoted himself to breeding unusual plants. On his brother Kurt's death in 1884, he joined the family firm and carried on his same work. This further solidified the company's reputation.

This all contributed to their remarkable success by the beginning of WW I. At the beginning of the twentieth century, they occupied extensive premises and employed nearly 300 people. That epoch was their peak. Franz Heinemann died on August 22, 1911. Friedrich Carl Heinemann, who had been wounded in WW I, died on September 20, 1919.

Franz Heinemann and his wife, Marie, had two sons: Waldemar, born on March 14, 1890, and Alfred, born on June 3,1892. Waldemar was called home from studying in England to run the family business in May 1911 due to his father's death. He continued on after his service in WW I, and in 1919 became part owner of the Heinemann company. After very challenging years, the firm began to revive.

As early as 1920, he was a member of Erfurt's commercial nurserymen and seed producer organization, as well as the German society of seed producers. In addition, he served on Erfurt's city council and also held an honorary position at the Reichsverband of German Horticultural businesses. Later, he held a number of volunteer positions in the Reichsnaehrstand (the Nazi government body in charge of food production), but according to many people who knew him, he did this only in the interest of Erfurt's horticultural community at the request of his colleagues. In 1938, he and his wife, Luise, traveled with Ernst Benary and his wife to the Twelth International Garden Show in Berlin, a somewhat risky venture for the Benarys in those days.

During the Third Reich the company focused entirely on vegetables, working closely with the Benary firm. They shared the same philosophy and both had highly skilled work forces.

The 1940 catalogue presented several thousand items. They were optimistic about sales. This was not to be. World War II was starting to affect the business. Crucial employees were called to the front. Then, in the night of July 8-9 1941, Allied bombs did a lot of damage to the tree nursery as well as to the glass covering the hothouses.

In spite of this damage, in 1941 they bought more land. On March 15, 1945, Waldemar's wife, Luise, lost her brother and sister-in-law in a bombing raid. As sole heir, she inherited the adjacent Franz Anton Haage nursery where her brother, Erich Wegener, had been manager and part owner. She and her youngest son, Franz Waldemar Heinemann (born in 1930), took over the management of this business.

While WW II had done relatively little physical damage to the Heinemann business, the biggest hardship resulted from the loss of employees who fell in the war, and the death of Luise's brother, Erich Wegener. The warehouse and an old barn stood there until 1946 when they had to be torn down because of war damage. The oldest of the company buildings, built in 1865, burned down in 1945. Hard times continued after the war's end, especially when Russian troops replaced the two-month-long occupation of the American Army.

After Waldemar, Heinemann and his family were forced to give up their home to the Soviets. They moved into their former residence at Kohlbrube, where they had to share the house with German refugees from further east. The Heinemanns were very generous in sharing whatever they had.

In January of 1946, Richard Spengler and Waldemar Heinemann, Rudolf Bulin, and the horticulturist Staendert, who worked in the Franz Anton Haage branch, were imprisoned by the Soviets. Waldemar Heinemann and Rudolf Bulin were released after several weeks, but the others disappeared and were never heard of again.

Waldemar was later murdered on January 21, 1947. Waldemar, together with his Italian driver, Gino Poli, and the general manager of E. Benary, Wilhelm Pfeil, had been driving back to Erfurt from a meeting in Quedlinburg. According to reports by Poli and Pfeil, the vehicle was stopped by uniformed Soviet soldiers who demanded fuel. After objecting, Heinemann was shot by the soldiers. Nobody ever found out what was behind the murder, nor was anyone ever held responsible for the crime.

By 1948, the year of the firm's 100th anniversary, things were better. Family members, 300 employees, and colleagues from Germany and abroad came together to celebrate Waldemar's legacy at the headquarters in the Weidengasse. The anniversary Festschrift also honored many longtime employees, including some who had died. Waldemar's nephew Alfred Heinemann took over the management, a position he held until his imprisonment in 1952. Heinemann was the victim of unfounded governmental persecution.

In 1952 Alfred Heinemann was taken away in handcuffs for questioning in Erfurt, where he remained throughout the trial that followed. Since he suffered from eye disease, he was handcuffed and escorted by guards to an ophthalmologist for treatment. The firm was accused of economic crimes, mainly for having sold small lots of seeds to West German customers who had accounts with F.C. Heinemann. Alfred was accused of "cheating" the government of the DDR. He was also accused of having founded an F.C. Heinemann GmbH in Hamm/Westphalia on December 5, 1947 to benefit Heinemann's. That branch went bankrupt on August 12, 1949, but Alfred was said to have continued shipping seeds to its customers without having registered these sales with the government. Another heinous crime was to have bought non-germinating seeds to grind into oil for their employees.

The punishment for these crimes was very harsh. Alfred was sentenced to ten years in the penitentiary and his assets were seized as well. This sentencing led to the expropriation of Alfred Heinemann's house. The newspaper gloated with hysterical headlines: "And Everyone Was Speechless," "Tough Punishment in the Heinemann Trial," and "The Clean Herr Heinemann and His Employees."

Alfred Heinemann stayed in a prison in Graefentonna until 1956 and then spent four more years in Waldheim before landing in a Leipzig prison hospital. Once that illness was treated he was released. Six months later, he and his wife, completely penniless, fled to a relative in Lippstadt (West Germany). Alfred spent the last nine years of his life in Lippstadt. He died on July 21, 1966. His nephew and heir, Franz Waldemar Heinemann, was neither allowed to visit his uncle nor to attend his funeral. Once Franz Waldemar's mother died in 1959, there were no more family members in Heinemann's firm until 1972.

Under Rudof Bulin's direction, the vegetable crops increased considerably. Then new ornamental plants were added and included gesneriaceae, begonia, calceolaria, cineraria, heather, rhododendron, fuchsia, geranium/pelargonium, petunia, and primroses, as well as field summer flowers like snapdragon, asters, gladiola, dahlia, iris, stock, sweet pea, helleborus niger, delphinium, phlox, pansies, and verbena. New fruit varieties completed the selection.

Eberhard Czekalla was taken on to train employees. When Rudolf Bulin died in 1969, Czekalla was promoted to his position. Bulin had been a truly key figure.

F.C. Heinemann was fully nationalized in 1972, as were many other businesses. Seven years later the firm was dissolved as a result of the nationalization. The sole surviving shareholder, Franz Waldemar Heinemann, was devastated by his losses and never recovered. Visitors who walk along the Weidengasse or around the apartments at the Huttenplatz, the Nordhaeuserstrasse, and the Muehlhaeuser Strasse wouldn't suspect that this had been the home of one of the most successful Erfurt seed companies for four generations or that it had helped establish Erfurt's reputation as a city of flowers.

Hoffmann wrote that previous generations remembered it was possible to smell the flowers in parts of Erfurt during the summer. There were so many of them the fragrance carried on the air. It is of course no longer the case. There are similar reports of fragrance in Sicily in the 16th century, wafting into Palermo from enormous lemon groves throughout the countryside during blossom time.

In a thoroughly modern venture, Annegret Rose has been actively managing about a hundred and twenty hectares in the "Marbacher Meadow." She created an organic farm, including herbs and flowers for seed, and also uses the property to demonstrate the value of crop rotation. Annegret's firm Saatgut Rose is still in business but it remains an uphill battle. Land for housing is in short supply and there is little to be gained by maintaining Erfurt as a "flower city" beyond sentimentality. Horticulture currently has minimal support in Erfurt. (JMT: Klaus Hoffmann wrote this in 2013) In its place there is now the IGA Museum of Garden History. A museum is the sign that everything is dead.

## Chapter 6: Saxony-Anhalt, home of Quedlinburg

The federal state of Saxony-Anhalt has only had this name since 1946. Previously, the area was made up of principalities and dukedoms that belonged to different German kingdoms. Subsequently, until the beginning of the 20th century, the designations of Saxony and Prussia were used. The National Socialists turned it into the Provinces of Magdeburg and Halle-Merseburg in 1944.

After World War II, the Soviet Military Administration in Germany named this area the Province of Saxony, and in 1946, Saxony-Anhalt. The DDR preferred to call them the districts of Halle and Magdeburg in 1952. After reunification, the province became the federal state of Saxony-Anhalt. The region has often been called the "cradle of ornamental plant culture" in Germany. There is some validity to that designation. In spite of its superficially bland appearance, the pre-Harz plain has a lot to say for itself.

From countless pre-medieval archaeological findings, we now know that this region was densely populated very early. Valuable Bronze Age relics indicate a highly developed civilization. The

Carolingian ruling families, Billungs and Liudofings, have left traces indicating that it was an important center of power for the region. There are remains of early development in Quedinburg with dwellings, a castle, and abbey. These noblemen reported directly to the emperor and the pope.

Quedlinburg is first mentioned in 922 AD in old chronicles. Heinrich the First was crowned as the first German King at the Quitlinger Castle in 917 and buried there in 936. His son, Otto the First, 912-973, was his successor and later the first German emperor. Hoffmann believed the German kingdom was founded in Quedlinburg, but this is probably a myth.

Heinrich's widow Matilda, later canonized, founded a religious community for women to have perpetual prayers said for her husband's soul. The nuns also ran a school for noblemen's daughters. In 994, Emperor Otto IV delegated the rights to manage markets, coinage and customs to the abbey in his absence. At first the abbey was very beneficial for the town, but unlike in Erfurt it later became an obstacle. Neither bishops nor princes could make decisions about the abbey's holdings. It was protected by countless laws and owned a lot of the land. It also controlled five convents and countless villages in the area.

It wasn't until Napoleon occupied many countries in Europe, including Germany, that the existing structure was abolished.

All these changes in the region didn't stop at of the gates of the abbey's domain. The churchmen were affected too. Increasingly, a self-confident citizenry had emerged, with their own ideas about how their city should develop. They wanted education and trade so they could prosper. The medieval townscape reflects some of that energy.

The fundamental structure of a medieval city is still visible today. The tension between the feudalistic character of the abbey on the castle hill and the modernizing drive from the end of the sixteenth century and the beginning of the 17th century was felt sharply in Quedlinburg. That was partly what led to its agricultural and horticultural development. Quedlinburg and the region became famous.

With the collapse of the flower growing industry, Quedlinburg is using its "World Heritage City" status as a magnet for tourism. It has more than 30,000 residents and in 1994 received the title from UNESCO. The city survived the wars intact.

Quedlinburg sits at the northern border of the Harz Mountains. The highest peak in the mountains, the Brocken, reaches 1,141 meters, just under four thousand feet. This geological factor is helpful for farming. The winter is a little milder than elsewhere. It has slightly less precipitation than the average for Middle Germany and more hours of sunshine in

September and October, an advantage for crop ripening. The soil is mainly loess, a finely porous surface, blown in on the wind and held in place by clay and granulated calcium carbonate. It is ideal for growing crops but also susceptible to wind damage itself. The topography of the fields allowed growers to use very large fields. Another unexpected advantage of the region was the proximity of the growing areas to large towns that supplied extra labor during the harvest season. It was analogous to Londoners going to pick hops in the Kent countryside in the summers or French students crushing grapes in the vineyards.

The Thirty-Year War from 1618-1648 brought devastating consequences, in the cities as well as the countryside. The Quedlinburg Abbey was not spared. The consequences of the war, with its destruction, plundering, and famine, were significant. The land was laid waste. In addition, plague killed thousands. In the years that followed, the abbey tried to stabilize itself financially through the sale and lease of farmland, especially of garden areas surrounding the abbey's property. Even though the monks and nuns gave up some of their land, they still encouraged horticulture. The abbey supported the establishment of parks and the planting of trees, and looked after the green areas of the city.

One can still see the "Abbey and Priory Garden," "the Deanery Garden," "the Infirmary Garden," etc. A late corollary of the hard times with the abbey having to give up some land was that the citizens benefitted in the end by being able to rent or even own land, something they had never had a chance to do before. The abbey was satisfied with its end of the bargain. The monks paid no taxes on rental income. Finally, all these systemic changes led to archaic business practices being dismantled. This allowed farmers to expand production.

City archives show that during the following centuries, a total of sixty-seven Imperial Diets took place there. Not only the Ottonians but also the Salier and Staufer families resided in Quedlinburg and influenced the region. Quedlinburg had other claims to fame. The poet Johann Gottlob Klopstock lived there, as did Dorothea Erxleben, the first woman physician in Germany. She took over her father's practice when he died.

Two events indirectly related to the city also affected it strongly. After the 1807 Tilsit Peace Agreement, the city of Quedlinburg, which had been part of Prussia, was turned over to the Kingdom of Westphalia under the rule of Napoleon's brother. The results of Napoleon's continental blockade were soon felt when sugar beet imports came to a halt. This stimulated an increase in local sugar production and the demand for sugar beet seeds rose to a previously unheard-of level. Napoleon's army's victory march through Germany as well as other places led to the dissolution of the Quedlinburg cloister and the sale of surrounding estates, giving seed growers the opportunity to move in or to expand.

Quedlinburg farmers led in agricultural production because of they were not afraid to try new things, unlike so many very rigid, hidebound farmers. It took great courage to depart from accepted practice. There were no second chances if a crop failed. Better to stick to methods which at least gave you something rather than gamble on new highfalutin' ideas that ended up with nothing.

This forward development accelerated in the eighteenth century as did other types of science. New agricultural ideas were coming from the Netherlands and being accepted across Europe. Fundamental discoveries about the nature and properties of the material world also kept pouring in. Nurserymen, plant growers, and scientists all contributed to the growth and reputation of Quedlinburg, the Harz foreland, and its fertile plains.

The city's fortunes were to become inextricably bound up with the success of Gebruder Dippe, described in some detail later in this chapter. The Dippe brothers came on the scene in the mid-nineteenth century, later than the original founding firms, but their consistent and methodical approach to growing the seeds, selling them profitably, and building on that foundation to expand ever further through clever marketing was more or less unique in that period.

Gebruder Dippe was the largest employer in the town until well into the twentieth century. Not unlike Benary in Erfurt, Dippe built housing for their employees and offered them social welfare as part of the contract. It may have been very paternalistic but it worked.

Many other seed cultivating companies were founded in or near Quedlinburg between the end of the eighteenth century and the early twentieth century. Some believe that the rain shadow from the Harz mountains contributed to the land's fertility. A lot of the older nurseries kept records and could recall their history, but many did not survive the economic and political turbulence of the post-World War Two epoch. In the first years of the new Germany, there were only a very few small nurseries left in the Quedlinburg area.

Klaus Hoffmann recalled meeting a few other nurserymen from neighboring towns in an old pub called "Zur Sonne," where they gathered a couple of times a year at a reserved table. Each time he reported on new horticultural developments by the Quedlinburg and Erfurt VEGs, of which he was a director.

Because it was never bombed, Quedlinburg still has most of its ancient impressive office and residential buildings, as well as courtyards with beautiful gateways. The houses have gables with little hatches, through which they attached hooks with rope pulleys to haul the harvest into the upper stories for drying or storage. A few of these structures can still be found here and there. Hoffmann says he hauled sacks of raw materials into the upper stories of a storage facility himself this way from 1965-1972. In most places by then there would have been a crane to do that.

An important part of the horticultural history of Saxony Anhalt is the public rose garden, Europa Rosarium at Sangerhausen. Toward the end of the nineteenth century, the German Rose Society met in Gotha and was concerned about the continuing loss of significant roses. They decided to create a place in which all the known cultivars could be planted and grown. One of the of the leading figures of that society was Peter Lambert (1859 – 1939), a revered rose breeder whose roses such as 'Frau Karl Druschke' are still in commerce. He was the one who really pushed this idea, and in 1903 the garden opened.

At present the garden has 6300 known different rose cultivars. It is a formidable, world-famous collection visited by thousands of people every year.

During World War Two and the subsequent Socialist period very little was done to the garden. Everyone had much more serious problems to face than worrying about roses. Lambert's own nursery in Trier and all his roses were destroyed by the war. After the reunification of Germany, rose lovers wanted to restore the garden. It had been very badly neglected and many of the roses had died. The current collection is not completely identical to the original one, but in no way less illustrative of rose history.

## Early nurserymen in Quedlinburg

### Martin Grasshoff

Probably the oldest seed company is Martin Grasshoff's, first mentioned in 1771. They sold seeds for flowers and vegetables. Quedlinburg's reputation began to rise in part because of Grasshoff's activity. He owned the first greenhouse in Quedlinburg and built some sort of hothouse in the Probstei Garden.

The firm owned almost ninety hectares by the end of the 19th century, and even then had to lease a few more fields from time to time. Their reputation and that of the town was augmented later by their active presence at flower shows. The financial crash of 1929 forced Grasshoffs to close, but a relative, Alexander Grussdorf, reopened the business a year later. Once the last owner died during the early part of DDR rule, the business closed permanently.

## Johann Heinrich Mette

In 1784, Heinrich Mette started his nursery. The business grew rapidly. This success made him became a leader of Quedlinburg horticulture. Before that, he had leased the Dechanei Gardens and had used vacant lots in the center of town to produce his seeds. The next generation bought these leased lots and added more to them. The firm became known as Gebrüder Mette. Following generations expanded these operations even further.

Production was not limited just to seeds for garden plants. The company's real strength lay in raising its own varieties of sugar beets, wheat, oats and rye. These were sold all over Germany and abroad. It was only later, once Mette became solidly established, that they considered flower seeds. They began with a few *Reseda*—mignonette—the staple of Victorian gardens, as well as early forms of *Dianthus*.

By its fifth generation, Johann Heinrich Mette had nearly 2,000 hectares and was growing four hundred varieties of flower and six hundred types of vegetables, as well as important agricultural varieties of beet, wheat, and corn. Johann Heinrich was very thoughtful and made long-term strategic plans. He put specialized scientists in charge of skilled professionals.

In order to improve the quality of the sugar beets and develop new varieties, they set up trials in 1881. One of the important features of a sugar beet is its sucrose content, in addition to vigorous growth and resistance to disease. The higher the concentration of sugar in the root, the more valuable it is. World politics at the time made tropical cane sugar very expensive, so Europe turned to its old standby, the sugar beet. While beet sugar is very sweet, it does not have the pure white color of cane sugar but retains a faintly bluish tinge.

Hermann Heinrich Mette and one other family member ran the business in the 6th generation. The firm lasted until it was expropriated in 1945. The family fled to West Germany. Heinrich Mette died in 1945 as a prisoner of war in Reval, Estonia (now Tallinn).

The ruins of the Gersdorf castle and the nearby estate are reminders of the famous Mette company. It ceased to exist after being in business continually for more than 150 years since its founding in 1784. There will be more about Mette in the chapter on ornamental plants, but it is good to report that agricultural seeds are once again being grown in its fields.

## Gebrüder Dippe

Gebrüder Dippe got its start in 1850 because of the shortage of beet seed. Even the best efforts of Gebrüder Mette were not enough to fill the demand. The Dippes were destined to become significant players in establishing Quedlinburg as a major center for seed culture and horticulture.

*Bild 65:* Gustav Dippe

Gustav Dippe, 1824 – 1890,, one of the founding
brothers of Gebruder Dippe in Quedlinburg
Reproduced by permission: Klaus Hoffmann

Christoph Lorenz Dippe and his brother Gustav Adolf had been gardeners and seed growers in Quedlinburg at the end of the 18th century. They each owned small nurseries and worked hard to create a solid financial foundation. Then they pooled their resources to form a new business, Gebrüder Dippe (or Dippe Brothers). Many years later, in 1915, the name was modified to reflect its new structure, Gebr. Dippe AG.

As the town flourished, the demand for vegetables and flowers increased. Sugar beet seeds were also greatly in demand, especially after Louis Hanewald invented a better method of extracting the sugar in a Quedlinburg factory. Gebrüder Dippe supported technical improvement in equipment for sugar production. This was very clever on their part, boosting their beetroot seed business.

Customers came to the city from far and wide to learn about this new method and bought the seeds to take back home, leading to an even bigger market for the seed. The Dippe brothers cleverly made the most of these favorable conditions and created a highly successful business which they wrote about, showing an enterprising modern spirit and good managing skills.

The eldest brother, Christoph, died childless in 1863. His brother, Gustav Adolf but later known as Adolf, had three children who were all working in the family business by the age of 20. The eldest son, Carl, took over the cultivation of sugar beets. He was extremely skillful and propelled the company to new greater levels of seed cultivation. This in turn led to new varieties and increased yield. Carl's younger brother, Fritz, grew vegetables and flowers, all the while adopting some of his brother's ideas. Their sister, Anna, married an art and garden product salesman, Karl Esche, who soon took on the job of sales and marketing, thus creating an ideal management team.

By the time Adolf died in 1890, the company had increased its area of operations threefold. Roughly half of this land was used for seed culture, plus a small fraction for flower seeds, doubling an already huge area. At that time the company was the largest of its kind in the world.

Gebr. Dippe's grew seed on a gigantic scale at its peak. About 350 hectares of their approximately 3,000 hectares were used for growing flowers. China aster (*Callistephus chinensis*) and pansies (*Viola x wittrockiana*) were the most numerous. There were about 500,000 potted seedlings in hot houses or on racks, of which over 300,000 were stock (*Matthiolus*), 20,000 wallflowers (*Erysimum*), and 8,000 cinerarias.

One could only imagine the manual labor involved in transporting all these pots. From the vantage point of 2018, it is also staggering to imagine that they managed to keep track of all this inventory without computers. During his years as nurseryman in Erfurt and Quedlinburg during the 1970s and 1980s, Klaus Hoffmann remembered the lasting impression made by vast fields with flowers and racks filled with potted plants. Selma Kleemann noted in an old town brochure of 1898 how unimaginable it all was.

Gebrüder Dippe had become Quedlinburg's biggest employer. They built more than 350 red brick apartments for their workers, still known as "Dippe Hause." They set their opulently designed commercial, storage, shipping, and research buildings in parts of the city where they blended well with the structures around them.

The company's social consciousness was remarkable. They organized facilities for the poor, the sick, and orphans, and they were generous in their support of childcare centers and public schools. Ernst Benary did much the same thing in Erfurt for his employees. Both firms recognized the value of a stable, well-trained staff. Not long before their era, Robert Owen in Manchester had demonstrated the effectiveness of paying workers well and making sure they lived in adequate housing. His cotton business soared.

Dippes' success drove the development of the city of Quedlinburg. The company needed to transport an increased number of large containers of seed in the 1860s. The solution was a branch railroad line. The line made it possible to trade with the rest of Germany and export seeds to other European countries and beyond. Dippes' Quedlinburg station was still visible in the 1980s, even though all transport of seeds had ceased by then.

The Dippe family began to expand into the surrounding area as it grew and opened branches in three different cities: Halberstadt, Neundorf/Anhalt, and Oschersleben.

Adolf Dippe turned out to be an exceptional person. He understood that it was important to improve the quality of the sugar beet seeds and employed scientific consultants to help him. Dippe built laboratories to test seed germination and the sugar level of the beets grown from his seeds. His efforts marked the beginning of scientific methods in horticulture in the last quarter of the nineteenth century. This required vision and money to build the proper facilities. Testing and selecting individual plants, understanding their lineage, using only tested stock for cross-breeding—all these seemingly simple notions started in Quedlinburg with the Dippe Company. This took place before Gregor Mendel's work on inheritance was rediscovered, and they had no way of knowing what the underlying processes were.

Over time, these improved practices benefited other companies too. Similar ideas were becoming more widespread. In Detroit, Dexter Ferry understood that inadequate germination was one of the main reasons he lost customers in his seed store. They felt cheated. He made it a rule to throw out all unsold seed at the end of the season and only stocked fresh seed each year.

As a reward for these outstanding social, business and technical contributions, Kaiser Wilhelm ennobled the Dippe family in 1901. For almost the next forty years, Dippe's reign was undisputed, though no doubt the First World War took its toll on their men and business.

After the Second World War and with the onset of Communist restructuring and Soviet influence, the family business, together with all those of the other big seed producers, was expropriated. Their choices were bleak. They could flee to the West or suffer further arbitrary repression.

Older residents of Quedlinburg can remember the huge Dippe Company plant. In the town itself, the main complex with its once attractive, solid buildings is now deserted. (Author JMT: this comment was made in 2013) Some of their buildings were put to other uses, according to Klaus Hoffmann. The Institute for Plant Cultivation and Research took over the Dippe bank under the DDR, filling it with laboratories and offices. The Institute continued on after the reunification, but once it moved into a brand new complex, the only thing left were sad, empty spaces with an uncertain future.

Today, there is nothing left of the world renowned Gebr. Dippe Company, neither of its headquarters in Saxony-Anhalt nor of branches founded in 1946 in Herford/Westphalia, and in Hilleshoeg, Sweden. Competition from all the other European companies was too strong for them. The last Dippe managers, Hans V. Dippe and Carl Esche, both died during the war and none of their heirs wanted to work in horticulture. A fitting tribute to the company founder, Gustav Adolf Dippe, is to be found in Quedlinburg's Wiperti-Cemetery where his gravestone has been restored and is well maintained. A new firm, Vertriebs Gesellschaft Quedlinburger Saatgut mbH, is now the successor to Gebruder Dippe, producing flowers and vegetable seeds in Quedlinburg.

## Smaller firms

### Gottlieb Samuel Roegner

Roegner was a very early commercial nurseryman in Quedlinburg, from about 1792 to 1845. His premises were at Abtei- and Probsteigarden and his mailing address was "vor dem Neuwegerthore." Gustav and Christian Dippe both built houses on this land in 1875.

### Samuel Lorenz Ziemann

Samuel Lorenz Ziemann, son of a Quedlinburg gardener who worked in the abbey grounds, founded his own nursery in 1788. He came onto the scene as a grower of flowers and produce, but with the demand for agricultural plants, he started to grow sugar beets for feed. In the beginning he just leased the land, but he, or more likely his son, bought the land in 1827. Ziemann's grandson, Carl Sperling, took over in 1913 and changed the name to Carl Sperling & Co. Its end in 1945 was completely predictable. The business was taken away from him, and the family fled to the West.

One reason so many highly trained German gardeners immigrated to the United States in the latter half of the nineteenth century was they had no hope of ever obtaining enough land to start their own business. Once in the United States, they showed what they could do. As note previously Georg Ellwanger, born near Wurttemberg in Germany, went into business with the Irishman Patrick Barry in 1852 in Rochester, New York and demonstrated that skill and mettle by creating the leading nursery in the country. They even sent plants to California, three thousand miles away, as the population exploded with the gold rush.

### Daniel Kettenbeil

Daniel Kettenbeil founded his nursery in 1793. He produced primarily flowers and vegetables. The rather small nursery was on the outskirts of Queldinburg but was protected by the west side of the town wall. Kettenbell was not afraid to move in new directions. He used greenhouses to grow pelargonium and later begonia hybrids, and became known as a courageous pioneer who introduced new varieties of flowers and other ornamental plants, thus making a significant professional contribution to the field of horticulture.

### Andreas Keilholz (1822) and Gebr. Laux

Andreas Keilholz (1822) and Gebr. Laux ran the Haan/ Rheinland Laux business' only branch in Quedlinburg. After 1945, their fields and buildings were handed over to two companies: P. J. Schmidt and Haake & Co.

## Hermann Wehrenpfennig

Hermann Wehrenpfennig started his company in 1876. He grew plants both in the open air and under glass. This company was known for cyclamen seeds and seedlings. Wehrenpfennig constructed greenhouses of astonishing quality and size for the time. They caused a sensation with one a hundred meters long. (This degree of excitement is surprising. The much larger Crystal Palace had been built twenty years before). The city listed this greenhouse for historical preservation but it was later silently torn down together with the whole nursery.

Working conditions in that building were deplorable. There was only one way in and out, a single entrance and exit. Klaus Hoffmann remembered the workshop areas. They were stifling. The building was modernized in 1975, but there were no changes in the layout. Greenhouses need proper ventilation or they become dangerously hot.

Their premises were handsomely landscaped with their own plants. Wehrenpfennig catalogues showed the possibilities for enhancing private gardens as well as public parks, a good marketing tactic. In 1952, the owner of the Wehrenpfennig

Company had fled the DDR and the Teupel Company took over the business.

## David Sachs

David Sachs founded his own vegetable and flower seed company in 1878. Sachs developed the 'Saxa' bean, which is still sold today. It was a successful business. When Rudolf Schreiber and Sons took it over in 1933 it became the third-largest seed producer in Quedlinburg.

Schreiber managed to avoid the all-too-familiar fate of most of the others. Their premises, Kleers Garden and parts of the Lindenstrasse, were used for plant production by the newly formed Erfurt VEG Seed Propagation of Ornamental Plants. This has now all been replaced by apartment buildings.

## August Teupel

Not to be forgotten was the nursery founded by August Teupel in 1880. He too built large greenhouses. They produced flower seeds as well as seedlings. Some of their more prominent lines were rex begonias, pelargonium and fuchsia. Of course it was Quedlingburg, so they also produced beet seedlings. Teupel became a leader in developing and introducing new varieties of ornamental plants. The owners left the DDR in 1960 and the company was managed by a trust.

## Sattler and Bethge

Sattler and Bethge was founded in 1881 and was later taken over by the Wehrenpfnnig company. The growers and seed producers were Carl Beck, Alfred Dillige, and Otto Storbeck. All tried to remain independent in the immediate post-WW II years.

## Other nurseries

Hoffmann recalled a number of medium-sized nurseries in Thuringia which also participated. W. Dietzmann in Zoerbig voluntarily joined the Quedlinburg VEG and produced pelargonium and fuchsia seedlings in a large greenhouse. The glass was in a deplorable condition and required constant repairs. All this became difficult to coordinate because of the distance between Zoerbig and Quedlinburg.

In 1969, the Quedlinburg open-air seed growing operation added two new companies, Haake & Co and Storbeck and Dannemann (from Weddersleben) to the co-operative, which became known as the "Kooperationsgemeinschaft Quedlinburger Zuchtbetriebe" (Quedlinburg Plant Breeders Cooperative). The resulting increase in land made it easier to implement modern technology. Although there were so many different growers, they seemed to cooperate quite well.

Once the state took everything over in 1972, the August Bebel VEG took charge of the cooperative in 1974. The whole Quedlinburg VEG Ornamental Plant Seed Growers of Erfurt was assigned to the August Bebel VEG in 1979.

The demolition of the obsolete facilities began in the 1980s and continued until the beginning of the 1990s. None of the facilities that had been brought into the cooperative exists anymore. Quedlinburg's growing grounds and greenhouses were all taken down and replaced with apartment buildings and new roads. Its worldwide reputation in horticulture had already begun to fade after the war. Now, except for a few historic markers and street names as reminders of the past, very few flowers are grown there now.

P.J. Schmidt's nursery remained independent and survived the DDR era without any difficulty. Perhaps there was some slight exchange of emoluments with a well-disposed official. The company still operates under its former name of P.J. Schmidt

In 1990, D. Schmidt started the meristem and tissue culture lab In Vitro Plant Service. While in another state-run organization for perennials in Quedlinburg, he worked on the propagation of perennials and orchids. He made this service available to the other local nurserymen. After 1990 this organization became Floraque Stauden & Zierpflanzen e.G. (Floraque Perennials and Decorative Plants).

Quedlinburger Saatgut GmbH, Satimex Quedlinburg Handelsgesellschaft mbH, and H & W Saatzucht Quedlinburg GmbH all arose from former state run Quedlinburg seed collectives.

After reunification, the property of all the private firms which had joined the VEG Saatzucht August Bebel was turned over to the German Democratic Republic's Treuhand (Public Trust). A Swiss company, Mauser, bought land and buildings in an attempt to recreate Quedlinburg's former seed producing industry, but it ended in liquidation. The fate of these places is still up in the air. (JMT: Klaus Hoffmann's narrative conveys this impression.)

Staudenbetrieb (Perennial Nursery) Weinreich in Wolmirstedt in Saxony-Anhalt and a few in other cities and regions have survived intact. It was a very productive member of the Quedlinburg GPG. The original owner was able to get the business returned to him in 1989, and now runs it under the name Floragarten Weinreich.

## Gotha

The only other time Gotha had star billing was when the Princess Victoria married Prince Albert of Saxe-Coburg-Gotha in 1840. If it had not been for the British public's anti- German hysteria during the First World War, Saxe-Coburg-Gotha would still be the name of today's English royal family. The Kaufmann Nursery in Gotha was active until the end of World War Two.

## Weimar

The R. Weizel firm later became B. Weizel and then B. Bielefeld. Under the DDR, countless firms in the city were combined into the GPG April 11th - Weimar.

## Kostritz

Christian Keegen and Panzer were well known for their dahlias. At the local Kostritz college courses in horticulture became available from 1886 to 1945. This was a useful source of well trained employee for nurseries in that area.

Countless other nurseries were busy before 1945 in Altenburg, Nordhause, Arnstadt, Mühlhausen, and other towns. Today they have all gone.

## Chapter 7 Saxony

Horticulture in Saxony evolved differently from Thuringia and Saxony-Anhalt. The complex effects of major religious institutions were not paramount as early as in the other states. There was also a greater variety of plants available than in the neighboring states. It is hard to tell whether this was because of special consumer tastes or because of the flexibility of nurserymen.

Christianity took root in Saxony considerably later than in other Middle German states. While the first gardens were being planned in 12th century Erfurt or Quedlinburg, the Meissen/ Dresden region was still having to defend itself against Slavic invaders. Heinrich I successfully named himself as duke and then as the first German king, and set about securing the borders of East Saxony with the building of a wall. In response to these intruders, the first castle erected was in Meissen where the current Albrechtsburg stands on the Elbe River. Counts ruled the land, followed by dukes, princes and electors, and then Saxon kings.

With increased security, monasteries were built and with them came a denser civilian population. That led to skilled handicraft and flourishing trade by the fifteenth century. A middle class, striving to emulate the nobility, began to take root. In Saxony this natural progression was in step with feudalism and a middle-class population.

In 1046, the Wittiner family gained power in Wettin an der Saale. They were the ones who prevailed in the establishment of Germany's first republic, the Weimar Republic, and strongly influenced the history of Saxony. What was impressive about Saxony was the continuous development in a variety of fields, especially mining, science, and art, as well as horticulture. The last was closely connected to the life and influence of the House of Wittin.

The family was ambitious in its involvement with politics in Germany, even when it meant taking great risks and suffering defeat. They were motivated by a strong desire for pageantry, for everything material as well as ideal. It seemed as if all the different classes of society shared this same desire. Part of pageantry was an elegant landscape. Court gardeners wanted to please the nobles with their work but there is little documentation about the gardens they created.

The nobility often got involved with the planning of gardens and parks. One example was the elector Moritz. He ordered his men to build Zwinger Gardens during his rule (1541-1553). His successor, August of Saxony who ruled from 1553-1586, ordered the creation of the "Herzogin Garten", (Duchess's Garden).

Dresden's parks and gardens bear testimony to the Wittin family's interest and example. This greatly influenced the developing middle class who didn't want to be left behind. They wanted to have gardens and plants. Then, as tastes became more refined, they increasingly wanted unique ones.

## Dresden

## Johann Heinrich Seidel

The climate of the Elbe Valley proved to be favorable for horticulture. In addition, the influence of Johann Heinrich Seidel was critical, not unlike that of Christian Reichart in Erfurt. Seidel lived in Dresden from 1744-1815 and worked as a court gardener under the Elector August III. After 1806 he worked for the king of Saxony.

Johann Seidel, 1744 – 1815, founder of the Seidel nursery

Reproduced by permission: Klaus Hoffmann

He showed just what he could do with the "Herzogin Garten." He was very highly regarded by the court. It wasn't only his intelligence and success with plants that made him outstanding, but also his horticultural knowledge and ability to find "unique" and unusual plants. Seidel collected as many as he could and grew them in his nurseries.

Seidel corresponded with other gardeners beyond Saxony, such as France and England. Goethe paid him several visits and admired Seidel's very well-organized plant collection. Goethe shared his own horticultural experience with him. Seidel not only had an enormous number of shrubs and trees but also understood their care and culture. He did amazing things with camellias and got dozens of them to bloom.

The story of how Seidel came by his collection is also fascinating. His second son Jakob Friedrich had been in France, working at the Jardin des Plantes. What follows is probably apocryphal but when it came time to leave he took (stole?) three of the royal camellias with him in his backpack.

Enough survived the long journey home to give him his start. He made it as far as Erfurt, but later used this stock to start his own nursery in Dresden. Part of the myth has it that the French police were out searching for him. Camellias had come from China and Japan and were established in France but had not yet reached Saxony. They were very valuable.

This event is often regarded as the birth of horticulture in Saxony. Camellias were reproduced by vegetative propagation. There were said to be over a thousand different species of them. That is highly unlikely.

Seidel shared his knowledge with other gardeners and taught his own children. They in turn followed in his profession. J. H. Seidel died in 1815. Six of his ten children became professional horticulturists. Two sons, Jakob Friedrich and Traugott

Leberecht, started a nursery, first on leased land and later on their own, a camellia nursery in Laubegast called T. J. Seidel.

The Seidels sold their wares all over Europe, even as far away as St Petersburg. This is a remarkable achievement. Keeping plants alive over long distances and through various kinds of weather was a real triumph. As if all that were not enough, Jakob Friedrich Seidel, now known as "Kamelliaseidel," also started to work with azalea and field-grown rhododendron. He was the first to do this in Germany.

The firm grew over several generations into a large-scale operation and had to expand. They bought additional land and set about producing 200,000 camellias, 175,000 rhododendron, and 150,000 azaleas in 1889. Eight years later in 1897, they moved the rhododendron production to new premises in Gruenbgraebchen.

Later the two nurseries split. The Laubegast division was expropriated in 1946. After being in business successfully for 133 years, there was no longer a T. J. Seidel company in Dresden. It became part of the VEG Ornamental Plant Seed Production in Erfurt, had to undergo necessary repairs, and was then used for the cultivation of a variety of ornamental plants.

The Gruengraebchen division continued doing well with rhododendron production until 1945. The owner never returned from the war, so his son-in-law, Ludwig Schroeder, took over as manager. His son, Christian Schroeder, is now the owner.

### Saxon nurseries

One of the unique things about Saxon horticulture was the great number of nurseries. There were said to have been more than a thousand of them before the second world war. Hoffmann thought that nine hundred were still active by 1992. One would have to verify that statement. If true, the Saxon horticulturists seemed to have managed very much better than those in Erfurt and Quedlinburg. The so-called "Saxon" cultivars of camellias, field rhododendron, azaleas, and later of heather were concentrated in and around Dresden and Leipzig.

The Elbe Valley with its mild climate is particularly well suited for growing these cultivars out-of-doors. Around Leipzig, the climate is only part of the story. The soil is particularly good in the nearby glacial valley left over from the ice age. It is light and slightly sandy, not heavy with clay. It thus drains well. The slightly acidic soil also suits rhododendron well.

The demand for these shrubs grew astonishingly quickly. This can be attributed to their many positive qualities, such as the beauty of the blossoms, their shape and color, their variety of shapes, their versatility, their durability, and their transportability. Many are also fragrant.

It was not surprising that floriculture grew so quickly during the nineteenth and twentieth centuries. One new nursery followed another in the areas around Dresden and Leipzig. Only a few were in the city itself.

The nearby meadows were initially leased and later bought outright by established and prospective nurserymen in the nineteenth century. With increasing demand for building lots, the nurseries moved out even farther from the city limits. The original land could be sold for a decent price in order to build a larger and more modern facility. Today when Dresdeners talk about Striesen, Laubegast, Gruna, or Strehlen, they are referring to little village-like settlements on the outskirts of the city which were incorporated into the city itself at the end of the twentieth century, built up around the old nurseries.

Julius Schaeme, Hermann Simgen and Heinrich Mueller owned some of the earliest nurseries. One of the most significant businesses was that of the Ruelckers (see below), but Elsner's may be the best known.

## Wilhelm Elsner

Elsner is known worldwide. The firm began in 1889 as a vegetable and field rose nursery. The first Wilhelm Elnser took advantage of all the new improvements which were coming online. He bought the earliest cold frames. He modernized and enlarged his greenhouses, allowing him to specialize. Their first seedling catalog was published in 1926. That was when he began to focus on pelargonium. The firm continues with extraordinary success to this day.

Some greenhouses were equipped with special lighting. In the 1960s, mobile irrigation systems were installed in the propagation houses as well as a lighting system for growing chrysanthemum parent plants. After 1956, a laboratory was set up for meristem and plant tissue propagation and for the examination of viral and bacterial infections in plants.

Later, for the first time, German scientists developed the use of heat to rid parent plants of pathogens. The laboratory where this work was done was expanded and modernized. About forty members of the Elsner workforce used this new facility in 1990.

In the 1970s, it became possible to manage temperature and airflow in the greenhouses electronically. Elsner installed one of the first indoor sunscreens at the same time. The company's insistence on top quality resulted in high demand, not only in the

DDR but in foreign countries as well. Even so, the government took over the firm in 1972.

Wilhelm Elsner 1921 - 2013  Owner of PAC Elsner, Dresden  Reproduced by permission: Klaus Hoffmann

Wilhelm Elsner, grandson of the founder, successfully ran the family business as part of the VEG Ornamental Plants Dresden for eleven years. After his departure from the company in 1983, he became a member of the VEG Seed Production of Ornamental Plants Dresden, which was established in the same year. In 1991, Elsner was able to get his business back from the DDR Treuhand. He renamed and managed it as Elsner PAC Jungpflanzen Dresden (Elsner Seedlings Dresden). "PAC" refers to the original concentration on pelargonium, anthurium, and chrysanthemum by his forebears. Wilhelm Elsner continued to insist on all his employees being well-trained and only introducing plants of the highest quality. Once again, this paid off handsomely.

Many of the former employees were still on board and his two daughters helped with the management. He retired in 1999, turning his business over to the fourth generation, his granddaughter Antonia Feindura and her husband Martin. Between 2002 and 2013, the new owners expanded their production on a five-hectare glass-covered facility in Thiendorf, about 25 km north east of Dresden. The State of Saxony gave Elsner a very good deal on the land. Both Hofmann and Elsner's family say he practically never referred to those difficult times in the 1970s and 1980s. He would only say there had been a bit of trouble when asked.

Klaus Hoffmann stayed in touch with Elsner over many decades. They first met in Quedlinburg and later Mittelhausen. After holding several other important positions, Hoffmann became the manager of the Elsner company in 1989. He stayed until 2003, coping with the transition to a free market system. His son Christoph also became a horticulturist.

The state horticultural society tried to organize an entire horticultural development comprised of many nurseries, but unfortunately this proposal was not met with enough enthusiasm. Today, the Elsners have moved their parent plant production out of Europe and into warmer climates. The seedlings are still grown in the modern propagation facility in Thiendorf. Wilhelm Elsner died in 2013.

### Ernst Ruelcker

Founded toward the end of the nineteenth century in Strehlen, Ernst Ruelcker's nursery became successful early on and survived not only both world wars but also the DDR as part of a cooperative. The Ruelcker company was restored after reunification and is currently run by the fourth generation. Growing a wide range of plants, Ruelcker is extremely effective at retail.

Now over a hundred and fifty years old, the nursery is one of the oldest in the city still in business. The way they managed to keep going and even prosper is very instructive. Ruelcker always thought through whatever he was going to do very carefully and left very little to chance. He focused a lot on new developments in horticulture, but avoided growing untried and risky new stock on a large scale. It was important for the company to exchange information with other professionals and businesses. This was evident in their participation in trade shows and the way they compared their own achievements with what was going on in other companies. All this allowed them to navigate the manifold difficulties around them.

## Robert Hoffmann

Robert Hoffmann was the founder of the Hoffmann horticultural dynasty. From its beginnings in Geisingstrasse it grew into an exemplary nursery. The Hoffmanns were active in various horticultural societies. When the DDR government ordered the formation of specialized state cooperatives, Robert Hoffmann was a pioneer and started one of these first state-run organizations. His youngest son, Guenther Hoffmann made a lasting mark with his indefatigable energy.

Instead of going into the VEG, Guenther went to work for Wilhelm Elsner, but later became the director of the VEG Seed Cultivation of Ornamental Plants. After reunification he took over parts of the VEG in a private capacity, but died too young at the age of sixty. Parts of his family's land became building lots.

## Max Ziegenbalg and Hermann Wirth

Ziegenbalg and Wirth started a horticulture business together in 1888. They produced potted plants like cyclamen, primroses, palms, and araucaria, as well as mayflowers and violets. Wirth retired soon afterwards and Ziegenbalg bought a larger facility in Laubegast/Leuben, where he started a brand-new nursery. It was very modern for its time.

The first thing Ziegenbalg did was to simplify steps in the production process, like watering and moving plants, as well as protecting them from frost and direct sun. The new complex was well laid out, with distinct areas for sales, production, utility and offices. The modern greenhouses were properly adapted to the growing requirements of the plants. Hoffmann visited this nursery at the end of the twentieth century.

Ziegenbalg became internationally known. They expanded their stock and sold many plant abroad. The company grew azaleas, heather (including the very first cold hardy variety, calluna), boronia, ardesia, and countless other cultivars.

Max Ziegenbalg contributed to the growth of horticulture in Dresden and was chair of a former professional horticultural society. Until 1945, his company was an important business model. The city's bombing in February 1945 caused heavy damage to their nursery. The company's success barely lasted two generations.

After Max Ziegenbalg's death, his two sons, Rudolf and Conrad, took over the business. Rudolf died in 1945, and when Conrad returned from being a prisoner of war in Russia in 1946, he took over the running of the company before he was incarcerated and condemned in one of Walter Ulbricht's DDR "show trials."

No crime could be found that he might have committed. Newspapers noted the chilling comments of Ulbricht's feared attorney, Hilde Benjamin, in the trial transcript: "You must be able to come up with some crime he committed." In spite of none being found, he was still convicted and exiled to West Germany. He died in 1957.

With all this going on the nursery was ruined by neglect and eventually the land was sold for development. After 1990, some of it was restored to Ziegenbalg's heirs.

## Arthur Voigt

Voigt started his nursery in 1895 after his apprenticeship and important years of learning abroad. He grew camellias, azaleas, roses, and hydrangeas but specialized later on in just azaleas, becoming an important grower of different varieties. With a total production of 300,000 azaleas and 50,000 heathers in the 1930s, he was among the biggest growers of these cultivars in Germany. At that time his facilities were very modern starting with his greenhouses. He even had an internal light railroad for moving the plants about.

After his death in 1940, the business went equally to his two sons, but in 1945 one of them left for West Germany. He had been forced to hand over his share to the DDR government. It later became part of the VEG Ornamental Plants Dresden. The other son, who was able to keep his share of the business, joined the GPG co-operative "Azalea" which later became connected to the GPS "Floradres." Today, all the Voigts' land is covered with apartment buildings.

### Kurt Engelhart

Engelhart grew dahlias in Leuben. He chose an inauspicious time to start his business, 1914. He bred his own varieties of dahlias and did well enough to expand the growing area to three hectares, but during WW II he had to turn the land over to vegetables.

His son, Siegfried, took over the business after his father's death in 1958. Because of building requirements imposed by the city of Dresden, he was forced to move the operation to

Heidenau, a small town just outside Dresden where the family still breeds and grows dahlias.

## Other nurseries

Alwin Richter, Bernhard Lehmann, Oscar Lessing, Louis Geyer, and Friedrich Kuntze were all known for top-quality plants and new cultivars, such as bromeliads and palms.

Julius Schaeme started his business at the beginning of the 20th century in Weinboehla. His sons and grandsons continued in their father's tradition, raising a great variety of azaleas in large numbers. After his death, his widow married Reinhold Ambrosius, who continued the business.

There were a few other companies near the city limits on Grunaer Weg, such as Arthur Voigt, Robert Weissbach and Bernhard Haubold. The Findeisen family reclaimed its company in 1990, only to sell its land in a top location for real estate development.

## Wilhelm Meurer

Wilhelm Meurer founded his nursery in 1872. It was the first in Dresden to specialize in landscaping.

**C.W. Mietsch**

C.W. Mietsch was known for training young horticulturists. His pupils Rudolf Hauswald, Friedrich Funke, Karl Hemple, and Eduard Hetschold all started their own nurseries later on in Dresden/Radeberg.

Elsner, Laue, Boehme, Hauber, Schleinitz, and Schroen were all at one time based in Tolkewitz. Only a few of them are still in existence. Boehme, Hauber, and Schleinitz were sold after 1990 and turned into building lots. The only thing left of Boehme is the residence and brand-new florist shop. Elsner bought the Laue company and absorbed it into his business. Land belonging to the Schroen company was mostly taken over by the DDR and used for building apartments.

**Victor Teschendorff**

Victor Teschendorff acquired Bernhard Haehnel's tree nursery, founded in 1880, in 1904. He moved it from Strehlen to Cossebaude. After his death, his son-in-law, Paul Haehnchen, continued to manage the rose division. In 1972 it was taken over by the DDR government and absorbed into the VEG Tree Nursery Dresden.

Paul's son, Eckart Haehnchen, regained ownership of the nursery in 1990 and ran it as a garden center until it had to close due to the catastrophic floods in 2002. (165) Another rose grower in Gostritz, Albin Huck, was forced to join the VEG Dresden until the restoration of private property in 1990. At that point the land was sold for building purposes.

## Claus and Torsten Kuehne

A fourth-generation vegetable nursery owned by Claus and Torsten Kuehne from Dresden Omsewitz was active in the southwestern region of the city from 1899. In the 20th century, the Kuehnes added greenhouses and cold frames. They were so successful they eventually had 15,000 square meters, which lasted until reunification in 1989. The output of this private nursery was unusual given that it had survived the rigors of the DDR without building materials.

In 1990, the owner's son, Torsten, opened a GbR (a type of business entity) with his father. Production was gradually changed from vegetables to ornamental plants. Two years later he started cultivating seedlings. Due to lack of space, some areas had to be temporarily leased.

The Kuehnes moved the company headquarters to Weixdorf after buying a now-defunct company. They then bought another large nursery in Genthin in 2012 which included a big retail center. All this was so big the Kuehnes needed seasonal help to run the huge greenhouses. They introduced new hydrangeas, breeding from their own sources. In this way, Claus and Torsten Kuehne's company became one of the largest ornamental plant producers in Middle Germany.

## Pillnitz

The former royal court garden in Pillnitz, completed in 1918, had a choppy history. In 1922, it was a horticultural trade school and research lab for ornamental plants. Subsequently it was taken over by the ornamental plant department at the Humboldt University in Berlin Koepenick.

In 1962, it became the Pillnitz branch of the VEG Ornamental Plants Dresden. By 1966, when it was taken over by the VEG Ornamental Plant Seed Production Erfurt, the whole production facility was in such a deplorable condition that it was hard to get the work done. Several greenhouses were declared so hazardous they were fenced off and abandoned. The heating system was in a deplorable condition.

What was left of the nursery still produced the usual potted plants. Certain new plants were added. Gerberas were grown for cutting as well as seedlings. This flower has a very weak stem and needs some form of support once the flower is cut. *Saintpaulia* and *Streptocarpus* were also propagated extensively.

The company's status kept changing. First it was an independent branch of the VEG Ornamental Plants Erfurt. It changed to a division of the VEG Ornamental Plant Dresden organization, then in 1983 to a part of the VEG Seed Production Dresden cooperative. These frequent changes were of no benefit to the company, especially since they were accompanied by frequent changes in management.

### Further changes

Nurseries in Erfurt, Nieschuetz, Weizdorf, Pillnitz and Dresden/Laubenast were consolidated into yet another VEG in 1983: Ornamental Plant Seed Production Dresden. Consider this date: it would only be six years before the whole political structure crumbled, and yet the authorities were still floundering about and flailing at any chance to make things worse.

More companies from Tolkewitz were incorporated. The former Elsner firm, then nurseries from Meissen, Gostritz and Coswig, and two nurseries from Gruenberg and Wackwitz. They had been in a regional cooperative. This new VEG had an enormous amount of space, but it was old, poorly maintained, and impossibly difficult to get any work done.

**After World War Two**

Events in Saxony more than anywhere else showed that horticulture did not come to a complete stop under the DDR. It was still possible to make progress, but only with the utmost difficulty.

Not all of the nurseries folded after the war. Many of them were able to get by as private entities and are still in existence. Naturally, they were forced to comply with all the cooperative rules imposed by the politicians. The evolution of the cooperative companies and their status after 1989 will be described below.

**Dresden floriculture after 1989**

It took the DDR more than thirty years to work out a system which had a slight chance of success. By the mid-1980s, things were going along fairly well but it was all destined to come to a grinding halt. Although Erfurt and Quedlinburg have the long history and thus gravitas of the main story, it is clear that Dresden was no secondary player.

The GPG (horticultural collective) "May 8" in Stetsch was Dresden's first GPG, state-run horticultural production organization, formed in 1950. That was followed by the LPG (Landwirtschaftliche Produktionsgenossenschafte) Young

Vegetable Center, a state run agricultural cooperative for spring vegetables. This was modeled after the GPG (horticucltural collective), since so many members objected to the original statute of the LPG. Until the beginning of the 1960s, many of Dresden's nurseries joined cooperatives but quite a few still remained independent.

One party member explained: "In 1963, you just became an executive of your cooperative in order to be left in peace." Lots of members hoped that by being part of a big group, they would face fewer restrictions on their operations. There were constant organizational changes as well as liquidations. In 1973, the GPG "Floradres" was formed. It was a conglomeration of about twenty-five cooperatives, a positive development for horticulture in Dresden.

In a secret vote, a rare event at that time, Karl Rasenberger was named director and held that position until the cooperative was dissolved in 1989. Rasenberger was a graduate of the Engineering School for Horticulture of Dresden-Bannewitz. He then became a teacher and eventually director of this institution. He was well-known and respected in Dresden's horticultural circles. They elected him because he didn't own a nursery and could therefore be a neutral and independent leader.

Rasenberger was very good at solving practical problems. Under his leadership the GPG developed as well as it could. He allowed individual growers to keep their large variety of cultivars. His theory was that everyone should stick to what they knew best. Unfortunately, no matter how enlightened he was, the grim reality was the rule that everyone had to follow, namely to meet the demand for Saxon special cultivars, at home and abroad.

## Saxon Special Cultivars

The development of Saxon special cultivars reflects the work of a few companies: Reinhold Ambrosius in Weinboehla, Hermann Stahnke and successors in Radebeul, and Kurt Gruenberg and Ernst Risse in Coswig.

## Reinhold Ambrosius

Ambrosius produced more than 30,000 azaleas in the 1950s. Most of them were the result of successful trials. His most significant work was in breeding new cultivars. Ambrosius died in 1956. He was a giant in the German azalea world.

## Hermann Stahnke

The Hermann Stahnke nursery has a long and somewhat tortuous history. Hermann Stahnke founded it after completing a thorough training in horticulture. When he was still a young man, he took over a vegetable and flower nursery in Nieschuetz on the Elb outside Meissen. There was a huge market in this town at the time, in 1901. He specialized in camellias, heathers, and azaleas. Stahnke built up the business with his sons Kurt and Karl. By the end of the 1930s they had very extensive nurseries. The whole operation was of the highest quality.

The Russians seized the company at the end of World War Two without any compensation. Karl turned to a decrepit horticultural facility in Radebeul and gradually built up a business, which later became a member of the GPG "Roedertalblume" Radebeul. He left the cooperative in 1990, sold his business to building developers, and became one of the first nurserymen in Saxony to rebuild, in his case in Naunhof near Radeberg. Karl Stahnke's son-in-law, Landmann, and his family, now manage the new and successful operation. Their main products are azaleas, mostly exported to Sweden.

The residual Stahnke business became a VEG and after 1964 became a branch of the VEG Ornamental Plant Production Erfurt (later on, Dresden). They too mostly grew heathers, and azaleas in huge numbers. Most of their plants were earmarked for export to other BRD states and to Italy. After reunification, the Treuhand sold the business to a Munich developer. This firm leased out the land later on.

## Kurt Gruenberg

Kurt Gruenberg's nursery in Weinboehla, founded in 1925, was small and easy to take in at one glance. It produced sour cherries and vegetables, most importantly asparagus. Later on, he moved it to Coswig. In the beginning he stuck with his original crops, then built greenhouses and dedicated himself more and more to azaleas and heather.

In order to survive he joined the GPG "Coswiger Blume" (Coswig flowers) and later, in 1983, went to VEG Ornamental Plants Dresden. His great-grandson Thomas Gruenberg was able to get the business back in 1990. He concentrated on a good assortment of heather gracilis and heather carnea, as well as calluna. The wide variety of choice and the demand guarantee good sales. The company has done well.

## Ernst Risse

Ernst Risse started his nursery in 1889 in Coswig and grew camellias as well as roses and vegetables. In the 1960s, the Risse,

Rudolph, and Romer businesses were all obliged to join the local GPG. After 1989, they all returned to their former private existence. Risse is now in its fifth generation. They produce about 10,000 camellias and azaleas each year.

According to Hoffmann, they polish these plants up for trade shows but otherwise grow the typical assortment of German horticulture—plants for bedding and plants to hang on balconies. Hoffmann thought they needed to widen their horizons and risk more variety to make the best use of the improved greenhouses and the larger fields they had bought. (JMT: Klaus Hoffmann did not sound too enthusiastic about this firm for some unknown reason.)

**Back to the Dresden VEG**

After the above digression to explain the origin of Saxon special cultivars, let us return to the Dresden VEG under Rasenberger.

Rasenberger somehow managed to build efficient new greenhouses and encouraged the production of more adventurous plants, especially for cut flowers. He explained another tenet of his philosophy to Klaus Hoffmann: "Make sure you have solid basic knowledge and then be enterprising and flexible." This was valuable advice for anyone wanting to become a manager in this cooperative.

More new nurseries followed, with an emphasis on cut flowers, such as carnations, cymbidium and roses. Another one grew bromeliads. All these were subject to governmental regulations. Only a few plants were exempt.

In the 1980s, "Floradres" started a commercial cooperative division called "Centraflor." It had a wholesale division supplying seventy florists and was responsible for both publicly owned and cooperatively owned businesses. Centraflor managed the marketing of flowers and ornamental plants. Overall, the "Florades" cooperative was a pretty good enterprise. It always worked well with private nurserymen. In 1989 "Florades" employed 800 workers, including retirees.

After reunification, "Centraflor" became a superstore. It was subsequently sold to a flower auction house from the lower Rhine (NBV). The new owners built a very modern store on the outskirts of town right next to the Autobahn. What was left of the old "Florades" leased the three remaining cooperative-run businesses: in the Riekerstrasse, in Laubegast, and in Meusslitz, which had been operating as independent GmbHs. None of them could make it and became insolvent. "Florades" still has about

70 members and is financially sound, even without horticultural production.

Countless members demanded the return of their businesses after 1989. Some of them attempted to begin anew, as in the case of Fischer, Quosdorf, and Kalau, but they too succumbed to economic reality and sold their land to real estate developers. One or two others, Ruelcker and S. Polke/ K. Richter, did better and made a go of it.

### Woldemar Nicolai

Coswig was the home of another nursery founded in 1896 by Woldemar Nicolai. He started out growing orchids quite successfully, a project that his son, Gerhard, took over and expanded into orchid propagation and cultivation. Over 5,000 square meters were designated just for the orchids.

When Gerhard died in 1966, the operation went to his son-in-law, K. Menzel, who succeeded him. He attempted to build a very large orchid business, but this never came about because of the GPG takeover in 1973. Menzel was appointed director of this cooperative, but when it ran out of money Menzel escaped to the West. Part of his business went to the VEG Ornamental Plants Dresden for which there was never any explanation.

## Max Wackwitz

There were many nurseries around Meissen, two of which are worth mentioning. Max Wackwitz built his business for shrubs and foliage on a slope in the Spargebirge, a hilly area near Meissen. This large nursery was remarkable for its unique stepwise construction of glass-covered areas and work spaces.

The business was incorporated into the GPG "Coswiger Blume" in 1973, then became part of the VEG Ornamental Plants Dresden in 1985. This proved to be fortuitous because the VEG director was interested in maintaining Saxony's historic horticultural sites. He helped organize overdue structural repairs of this nursery. Wackwitz's son got the firm back in 1990 and is running it in the same way as his father, with the addition of peonies as cut flowers.

## Herbert Fichtner

Herbert Fichtner grew carnations as cut flowers and foliage under glass. When the business was expropriated in 1955, Fichtner left for West Germany and it became part of a VEG. There appeared to be a lucrative cut flower market in Meissen, so the authorities invested in a new greenhouse with a polyester cover and a coal heating system. The nursery burned 9,000 tons of coal a year. The resulting soot and air pollution enraged the neighboring residents. Not surprisingly, the business failed and was assigned to the VEG Ornamental Plants Dresden in 1985. Ham-fisted to the end.

After 1990, Herbert Fichtner's heirs got the business back but sold the land for development. The remaining structures were demolished. All that is left to remind anyone the nursery ever existed is a sixty-meter chimney used as a transmitter mast by Telecom.

More than fifty active growers concentrated on azalea and heather around Leipzig, in places like Hartmannsdorf, Holzhausen, Markkleeberg, and Baalsdorf. Many of these nurserymen fled to West Germany after World War Two. They started new businesses focusing on shrubs such as rhododendron. Karl Glaser and Max Friedrich Wolf made important contributions in this field.

All these nurseries were seriously damaged by the war and took a long time to become productive again. In 1950, thirteen businesses joined the Hartmannsdorf GPG (horticultural collective). It had a very good reputation and its plants were widely sold both within the DDR and abroad.

There was one bright spot amid so much dispiriting news. After 1990 this GPG became a registered co-operative of the West German type. The new business, Meyer/Engelange, built a very large new greenhouse and was managed by excellent staff from the former GPG. Later, Hans Mueller from Stuttgart-Kornwestheim bought the whole operation. He was a tree farmer. Mueller grew ground cover plants for residential and landscaping purposes and then leased the newer area back to the former owners. Somehow this melding worked, and both firms did very well.*

Generally, though, crop growing areas around Leipzig suffered tremendously from the war. The continued use of brown coal only added to the trouble. The quality of the plants did not meet West German standards. As is so many other places, there are hardly any more nurseries around Leipzig. The land has been used for road, real estate development, and strip mining.

*(Klaus Hoffmann's personal experience)

**Engler's**

Hoffmann liked this firm. Franz and Claus Engler, son and grandson of Engler's in Miltitz, navigated the difficult times quite well. The nursery had been founded in 1889 but somehow survived to supply Leipzig and foreign countries with young plants, particularly Lorraine begonias. Victor Lemoine had been the pre-eminent hybridizer in Lorraine and these flowers were very important. He only used the names of cities and states for his best cultivars.

Engler's seemed to indicate that a well-run company with a highly skilled team of professionals could still operate under the tough business environment of the GDR time, but there may have been something else at play. Similarly well-run businesses with equally high standards were destroyed for political reasons. Maybe the Englers played ball with the authorities in some way. This is pure speculation and not meant to impugn the present firm in any way, but remaining open and visibly successful was the exception, not the norm.

The workforce was well motivated and knew its stuff. The owners had organized the use of the greenhouses much more carefully than other businesses and were always on the lookout for new plants to grow and propagate.

While still in training, Hoffmann joined Engler's to learn more about Lorraine begonias. On another occasion, he visited Miltitz to see how they used cold frames for the Lorraine begonias.

There was also some talk about transferring parts of Quedlinburg's Lorraine begonia breeding material to the Englers. Erfurt horticulturists visited Miltitz to see the new conveyor-belt greenhouses. Contact continued when Hoffmann joined colleagues who went to Miltitz to ask about new varieties of *Saintpaulia* and tissue cultivation of lilacs.

## Baumschule Boenicke

Baumschule Boenicke was a highly regarded arboretum founded in 1876 in Delitzsch. They produced espaliered trees, but after World War Two, the business came to a halt. It was insolvent. A dentist from Delitzch with no horticultural experience decided to buy it. Before he could do anything with it, his involvement in persecuting Jews during the war came to light and the DDR expropriated his business. The government turned it over to a Leipzig VEG while the dentist fled.

The VEG moved into producing flower bulbs. It built new mobile greenhouses which were well suited for the bulbs. In 1965, it merged with the VEG Ornamental Plants Seedlings Erfurt and enlarged its capacities. Most tulips and narcissi were grown in the open, but tender plants like freesia, certain narcissi, and special tulips were under glass. All this was leading up to International Women's Day on March 8. They needed two million tulip bulbs for the occasion.

The research division of Humboldt University in Berlin-Koepenick set up a team to understand freesia better. Nurseries from the rest of the DDR ordered their spring bulbs from Boenicke. Many other nurseries tried but failed to grow bulbs *en masse*. The failure lay with ignorance about the plants' temperature requirements. High temperatures in May caused the leaves to shrivel prematurely, with resulting failure of the bulb to grow properly.

This failure was a classic example of the DDR's isolation preventing very skilled people from leaning better methods from other European countries. These nurserymen were perfectly capable of making things work if only they had the information.

As if all this were not enough, Delitsch's farms faced the encroachment of coal mining in the 1980s. Only reunification saved them. The premises were taken over by Selders from the Rhineland, which built a garden center and tree nursery.

## Klaus Dohrmann

Klaus Dohrmann's nursery in Goeben did become a victim of coal mining. They produced heather and cut roses. Because of being forced to move, Dohrmann rebuilt his business in Panitzsch just outside Leipzig using state subsidies. He specialized in growing roses. From then on, the business followed a familiar path. It was taken over by the government and then incorporated into the VEG Leipzig-Kleinzschocker in 1974.*

As a highly regarded manager and professional, he was able to keep the business afloat during the challenging time of the VEG Leipzig cooperatives. One initiative paid off, cut roses. After reunification, he and his family regained their business. Slowly, despite his age, Klaus Dohrmann built the rose stock back up by adding new varieties which he selected carefully. Unfortunately, his sudden death left the company without leadership. Attempts to restructure failed and the family was faced with insolvency. Everything has now been demolished.

(*Klaus Hoffmann's personal experience and conversations with K. Dohrmann)

## VEG Leipzig Kleinzschocker

VEG Leipzig Kleinzschocker was a big business. It was comprised of many divisions and produced a wide variety of plants. The VEG supplied Leipzig and the surrounding district with flowers. Some of the businesses that came under its umbrella were that of Max Friedrich Wolf in Markkleeberg, the former bulb nursery in Doebrichau near Torgau, a foliage and orchid nursery, a large greenhouse in Grosszchocher, and the rose nursery in Leipzig-Panitzsch. Very little of this conglomerate survived reunification. All attempts at privatization failed.

## Chemnitz

The winters are earlier and colder while spring comes later in Chemnitz. This meant that growing flowers had to be approached differently from other regions. Under the DDR, Chemnitz was known as Karl Marx Stadt, but the city reverted to its original name as soon as it could.

The colder climate reflects the surrounding Erzgebirge (the Erz mountains) and Vogtland. The countryside is very hilly, leaving limited open space. Chemnitz was industrialized very early, creating a large work force. This growing population meant that there was a market for many small nurseries in small towns offering an assortment of plants and flowers. None of these was noteworthy (according to Hoffmann).

The arrival of cooperatives didn't put a stop to these small operations. On the contrary, many very small GPGs sprang up, helped by the addition of new greenhouses. There were effective cooperatives in Chemnitz, Zwickau, and Plauen. *

* (JMT The great composer Robert Schumann, 1810 - 1856, was born in Zwickau)

All three cooperatives kept going until 1989. They provided the fresh vegetables and a wide range of flower and plants needed by the townspeople. Not only did they expand the growing areas, but they worked well with two different state organized co-operatives.

As we have seen before, none of this was any use in the end. All the greenhouses and surrounding facilities were eventually torn down. It was this reality in case after case which led to the dramatic drop in the former DDR's horticultural production mentioned previously.

**Emil Richter**

Emil Richter opened a nursery at the end of the 19th century. It became widely known outside Crimmitschau, its hometown. He produced a very wide spectrum of plants in his small nursery. His son, Walter, traveled widely and brought back many orchids and bromeliads from his travels and used them for propagation.

Right after the war, he had to take over the business and had no way of growing anything much except vegetables. A Russian officer who shared a passion for exotic plants helped Richter procure enough fuel to keep the greenhouses heated properly for his tender orchids and bromeliads. Richter liked to talk about his friendship with this officer, who returned home to become director of the Botanical Garden in Moscow. This must presumably be the same man who was so kind to Kakteen Haage in Erfurt. One can only imagine how clever he was to avoid all the possible fatal political collision points around him.

Walter Richter made a big contribution to the world of horticulture, both within and outside the DDR. He was admired for his modesty and willingness to share his knowledge with his colleagues. He documented his results and discussed them at his lectures. The other men appreciated his generosity. For many years he was the director of a special group of orchid growers.

The government appropriation of his business in 1972 was particularly tragic for him. He coped alone until 1983, but suffered from the clumsy interventions of ignorant new managers. He received several honors: honorary Horticultural Engineer from the Humboldt University of Berlin, and "Verdienter Zuechter" (Honored Horticulturist) by a government institution twice. Eventually the business was incorporated into the VEG Ornamental Seed Production Erfurt as a branch working on freesias and gradually faded from memory.

Sadly, Richter became blind in the last eleven years of his life. He died at 93. Luckily he did not undergo the collapse of his business. His daughters got the business back, but they too gave up growing flowers like almost everybody else. All that remains of a distinguished man and his life's work are a few ruins and a street with his name.

## Jehmlich Floristik e.K

The Jehmlich Floristik e.K nursery in Olbernhau/Erzgebirge was also well-known. It was started in 1874 and is still managed today by the fourth generation, Horst Jehmlich. The firm survived all the challenges of the past 140 years. It was known for excellent customer service and that helped a great deal. One of their best decisions was to concentrate on ferns. Very few other nurseries grew them. Because Jehmlich often displayed ferns at trade shows, they received many orders, even from foreign purchasers.

Amazingly, they kept their identity in spite of being part of a GPG. In the 1980s, Horst Jehmlich was named director of the GPG "Drei Tannen" but had to face a court hearing to phase out the cooperative. The business was returned to him in 1990 and his father was able to attend the company's 120th anniversary celebration in 1994. In spite of all the efforts he made, things did not work out and he turned to retailing.

Horticulture on a grand scale never played a big role in East Saxony. There were neither the right climate conditions nor the right demographic conditions to support a healthy market. Many small nurseries satisfied this limited demand. One established cactus growing operation was assigned to Michael Haude in

Jaenkendorf. It did not survive the reunification, leaving only an abandoned building behind.

There was the GPG Bautzen, a conglomerate of many small nurseries. In the 1960s the two cooperatives "Budissin" and "Morgensonne" merged, creating an important supplier of ornamental plants and tree nursery products for the whole region, including Dresden. H. Dienemann owned one of these businesses. The cooperative utilized extensive land for its crops and also had a few florist shops. It dissolved after reunification. The former tree nursery was returned to its former owner, Seemann, and is still very active.*

(*Klaus Hoffmann's personal experience)

## Chapter 8: Horticulture in Berlin

### Ornamental plants in Berlin and Surrounding Areas

There was much less horticultural development in and around Berlin than during the late seventeenth and early eighteenth centuries in Middle Germany. The main influence on horticulture in this area came from the Prussian nobility and a growing upper middle class. They laid out parks and landscaped their palaces and country estates.

Enthusiasm for parks and pleasure grounds started around the end of the eighteenth and beginning of the nineteenth century, and marked the birth of horticulture in Berlin. Peter Josef Lenne (1789-1866), who had an excellent education as botanist, gardener, and landscape designer, and who had designed and overseen the work on a large number of parks in Berlin, Potsdam, and an area north east of Berlin, led this movement.

He had worked with the brothers Andre and Gabriel Thouin in Paris, Ludwig Schkell in Munich and Geneva, Jean Nicolas Louis Durand, and also Prince Pueckler in Muskau. The latter was a most original and fascinating character. He spent almost more time in England and France learning about landscaping than he did on his estate in Muskau. He also desperately needed to raise money for his ideas. In a truly bizarre arrangement, he annulled his marriage so he could be free to marry a richer woman to finance his estate. He and his wife remained close and he was unable to find the heiress he needed. It was a great idea, though.

Friedrich Schinkel, renowned artist, architect and city planner, influenced Pueckler profoundly. In 1823 the Prussian

King Friedrich Wilhelm III named Schinkel director of the royal state tree nursery and the horticultural academy. In 1828 he became director of the royal gardens in Potsdam and Berlin. Berlin's Kaiser Wilhelm University created a department of agriculture with related natural sciences such as botany, plant nutrition, and genetics at the turn of the twentieth century.

World War II destroyed much of Berlin and its surrounding areas, resulting in the loss of many parks, nurseries, and large parts of the university's science buildings. These devastating losses did not erase the great scientific advances which had been made between the wars and it was certainly not by chance that Ludwig Spaeth's nursery on Berlin's Baumschulenweg, and later in Ketzin near Potsdam, had grown to be such a big business. It had been founded in 1720 and lasted until 1945. Spaeth started as a tree farm, and for a while it was the biggest of its kind in all of Europe. Only old John Veitch in Scotland rivalled them.

Spaeth took their cue from the early 19th century parks around the city. Successive generations of owners wisely chose committed innovative managers, had very well-trained employees, and a broad spectrum of reliable nursery stock. Due to the proximity to the university, there was an easy exchange of information about the best way to grow woody plants.

The company was able to keep going almost up to the end of World War Two. The last owner, Dr. Helmuth Spaeth, was involved in anti-Nazi activities. This led to his arrest in 1943. He ended up in the Sachsenhausen concentration camp and was shot to death.

The business was expropriated after 1945 and made part of a VEG tree nursery. Its grounds, styled after an English garden on the Baumschulenweg, are striking with nearly five thousand types of tree on about 3.5 hectares. The world-renowned dendrologist, Gerd Kruessmann, managed it until 1945.

**Karl Foerster**

Karl Foerster, 1874 – 1970, founded his initial perennial nursery in 1903. Foerster came from an educated family and learned the basics of horticulture in the Schlossgarten Schwerin. He followed that with additional horticultural education at the Potsdam-Wildpark Horticultural Academy. His first nursery was on his parents' land, but in 1911 he set up "Senkgarten," a new nursery on farmland in Potsdam-Bornim. This is the one which became legendary.

Karl Foerster, 1874 - 1970  distinguished Berlin horticulturist

Reproduced by permission: Klaus Hoffmann

Many artists, landscape designers, musicians and others were drawn together as a group called "Garden Design in Bornim" and settled in the area. Karl Foerster ran his nursery for perennials. Next to his now famous home, he artistically arranged areas for cultivating and propagating the plants. Because he bred new plants on a very large scale, he incorporated performance tests into his program. A big bed of his new plants was installed at Potsdam's famous Freundschaftsinsel, ("Friendship Island") in 1941.

The Friendship Island in the river Nuthe had been originally laid out by Schinkel a century before. In the 1930s, the authorities decided to change the city entrance from the Langen bridge and create a new entrance to the Residenzstadt. At first, they only modified the green spaces on the left and right of the bridge, with the Kaiser-Wilhelm monument on the southwest side. Then Karl Foerster suggested extending these plans in 1937 from the Sight Garden, and the area of the Freundschaftsinsel was integrated into a "flower garden of the future" up to the present island bridge.

Karl Foerster was an impressive individual. Hoffmann met him once while he was still a student. Horticulturist, plant breeder, and author of numerous professional books on perennials, grasses and ferns. Foerster was recognized in several different ways. Berlin's Humboldt University conferred an honorary degree on him. In 1955 he received the national achievement prize from the DDR. On his 85th birthday he was named an honorary citizen of Potsdam, and finally in 1964 he became professor emeritus at the Humboldt University.

His books, "Ferien vom Ach" and "Warnung und Ermutigung" reveal how Foerster saw life and his experience as horticulturist. According to Hoffmann, both books remain well worth reading and reveal a lot about what Foerster was like. In 2001, the "Bundesgartenschau" (Federal Horticultural Show) was held in Potsdam. They used the opportunity to recreate Foerster's planting design in the Freundschaftsinsel. At the show's opening, the display garden was open to visitors once again.

Why his relatively small business was taken over by the state after his death is still puzzling to Klaus Hoffmann. Unlike so many other nurseries, it was well run as a VEG and was one of the very few places to buy perennials in the DDR.

Hoffmann tells an intriguing anecdote about the VEG. The new manager, Paul Hahn, formerly director of the VEG Ornamental Plants Seedlings Erfurt and Hoffmann's superior, was penalized for some reason and transferred to Bornim. Hahn saw that his new workforce was very well qualified but they still adhered to old customs. Regardless of the anti-religious rules of the DDR, they gathered in the cafeteria and began every day with a prayer. Paul Hahn never took part in this and stayed alone in his office, a practice he never changed.

There is an amusing anecdote about Foerster. The well-known Irish garden writer Helen Dillon visited him in Germany while he was still an active gardener. He asked her to accompany him on his rounds as he checked on the results of his delphinium crosses. Mrs. Dillon reports that he was utterly ruthless, as only the great flower breeders can be. If a seedling did not meet his expectations, he smashed it to smithereens with his cane while his terrified garden assistant shrank into invisibility.

Berlin's main focus was politics, culture, science, and the organization of a steady food supply. At that time, almost all flowers and plants had to be imported. Several times a week a truck loaded with flowers from the Rhineland drove into West Berlin to the wholesale flower market in West Berlin after 1945. The orchid business "Valerius" produced special plants up to the 1990s, as did "Koelle" garden center.

Hoffmann draws attention to some of the successful twentieth-century nurseries in Berlin: Rothe/Grille, Golm, Fassbender, Imme, Brandt and Nette. There were also the Buchmann firm, still in existence, and Bergemann and Pluta. Hoffmann considered that horticultural development in East Berlin between 1950 and 1987 was remarkable, especially when compared to the development of similar specialized fields under the DDR.

He thought that there were at least three conditions that made this happen: Many East Berlin nurseries had lost their senior managers. The latter had fled to the West between 1946 and 1950. The businesses were then turned into the communal "Volkseigene Betriebe "(Publically Owned Operations). What made up for the lack of senior management was the assignment of enthusiastic young directors who were often graduates of the Humboldt University. The SED (socialist party of the DDR) made supplying East Berlin with produce and flowers a top priority. They built new greenhouses and provided more materials for production than they did in other parts of the DDR. At the same time, no one worried about the environment.

Finally, the horticultural department of' the Humboldt University had a pool of well-qualified graduates from which the new horticultural businesses could draw, as long as they were allowed to make independent hiring decisions. The young graduates also wanted to stay in Berlin while the university, and the nurseries cooperated well.

Most of the remaining nurseries were heavily damaged by the war and uneconomical to run. That quickly led to creating larger VEGs to try to overcome these disadvantages, for example the VEG Berlin-Weissensee, which the former Grille Brothers joined. The formerly private Franz Golm company from Kaulsdorf joined the VEG Horticulture Berlin-Rummelsburg. Later, the Fassbender company, which was part of the Treuhand administration, also joined it.

In 1961 another VEG was established, called VEG Horticulture Berlin-Lichtenberg which incorporated the abovementioned businesses that had survived up until 1960. In 1964, these three remaining businesses regrouped once again as VEG Horticulture Conglomerate Berlin. Cooperation between the businesses proved to be an excellent solution. With no competition between them, they shared the goal of turning out the best horticultural products they could.

Soon after this, the cooperative "Berlin–Flowers" was formed. It was an establishment comprised of the conglomerate VEG Horticulture Berlin and the GPG Horticulture Potsdam/Berlin. This laid a foundation for horticulture in Berlin proper as well as in its outlying areas, which led to successful operations up until 1990.

The horticultural conglomerate was very lucky to have Erich Steffens as its director. He was politically savvy, a well-educated professional, and a talented leader, all which made him a good manager. Klaus Hoffmann always admired the apparent harmony between those in charge and the noticeable freedom they were given for business decisions.

The business in Berlin had five divisions for horticultural production, a sixth for technical questions, and a seventh for cultivation and process technology. By the time the DDR collapsed in 1989, the operations had grown to cover twenty hectares of glass or foil-covered growing facilities.

One of these divisions grew interesting varieties of potted plants, such as bromeliads, *Anthurium scherzerianum*, cyclamen, and foliage plants (not particularly in the DDR), as well as some hydroponic plants. Another was involved in growing carnations, roses, gerbera, and alstromeria for cut flowers. They did interesting things with orchids. Cymbidium and phalaenopsis sell best, followed by paphiopedilum and oncidium. Great care went into raising healthy carnations, starting early on with intensive maintenance and attention to plant health. With meristem propagation, the availability of mother plants was guaranteed. Up to a million seedlings were grown each year.

A big division was built in Borgsdorf, home to horticulture since the turn of the century, dedicated to growing roses, carnations, and chrysanthemums. The carnations were grown in artificial media. Because of the division's size they were also required to grow a certain number of greenhouse vegetables for the Berlin market.

City planning necessitated moving the greenhouse facilities from the inner city to the outskirts of Berlin. A new greenhouse was built in Berlin-Herzberge in the 1980s. They grew the same cut flowers noted above. A very large glass-covered area was used just for cultivation and technical research, all tended by a team of twenty-five employees. A technical team was given its own workspace to come up with useful mechanization whenever possible. They developed irrigation systems, tillers for raised beds, and automated garbage removers.

Hoffmann thought that the Berlin greenhouse conglomerate was an excellent example of how, even in a communist-run country, there could be positive aspects basically once researchers, teachers and the workforce communicated well.

Professional training, whether horticultural, technical or artisanal, was of crucial importance. It was an absolute necessity for the DDR. At the time of the reunification the conglomerate employed about 850 people. Most had a vocational certificate, but fifteen percent had a university degree and seven percent of those were a masters or doctorate.

The collaboration between Humboldt University and other similar institutions was remarkably good. The workforce was similar in the other horticultural businesses outside Berlin as well as those in Berlin and Potsdam. Potsdam had the cooperatives "Bluetenfreunde Luckenwalde," "Immergruen Tetlow" in Trebbin, Felgentreu, and Jueterbog. Some of the Berlin cooperatives were "Kleeblatt," "Weisse Taube," "Bluehende Zukunft," and "Hermann Schlimme."

What became of these businesses after reunification? The answer is that they all came to naught. Even though the firm of Grille and Golm got their land back, they immediately sold it to developers. The Treuhand's (Germany's Public Trust set up to sort out the problems of reunification) premises were torn down and that land was also sold for building purposes.

The GPG facilities in Berlin and outlying areas were handed back to their former owners, but only a few returned to nursery work. Essentially nothing is left from either the publicly owned VEGs or the state-run GPGs. A new garden center, "Koelle," was built on the grounds of the former Borgsdorf business.

There were two exceptions: the GPG (horticultural collective) Langerwisch which was partly privatized and is now a rose nursery, and the GPG "Bluetenfreunde," now a nursery called "Mayer" that grows garden and window box plants. The GPG Felgentreu became a registered cooperative society (West German style).

PRESENT DAY (2017)
NORWAY
Oslo
SWEDEN
Stockholm
Helsinki
ESTONIA
Tallinn
RUSSIA
North Sea
Baltic Sea
Riga
LATVIA
LITHUANIA
DENMARK
Copenhagen
(RUSSIA)
Vilnius
Minsk
POLAND
BELARUS
NETH.
Berlin
Warsaw
BELG.
GERMANY
Quedlinburg
LUX.
Erfurt
Kiev
CZECH REPUB.
Prague
UKRAINE
SLOVAKIA
FRANCE
Vienna
Budapest
MOLDOVA
AUSTRIA
HUNGARY
Bern
SWITZ.
SLOVENIA
ROMANIA
CROATIA
Belgrade
Bucharest
Adriatic Sea
BOS. &
HERZ.
SERBIA
ITALY
MONT.
Sofia
BULGARIA
Rome
ALBANIA
MACE.
Black Sea
Istanbul
GREECE
TURKEY
Mediterranean Sea
Athens
0    200km
0    200mi
ALG.
TUN.

## Chapter 9: The value of basic science to horticulture in East Germany

A very important factor in the effectiveness of all these businesses was the embrace of basic science by commercial growers. At the beginning of the 20<sup>th</sup> century, departments of horticulture were created in universities, such as Halle, Berlin/Muenchenberg, and Goettingen. This was a somewhat revolutionary move. After all, horticulture is essentially a very practical profession, at first sight without much theoretical background, but the idea that genetics, cytology, biochemistry, botany, and plant pathology affected the success or failure of crops was rapidly emerging.

Some years earlier, in the early 1870s, the first professor of agriculture at the brand-new University of California three thousand miles away, Eugene Hilgard, believed this was true too. He father was a German political refugee who fled Germany after the 1848 uprisings and took his great learning to America.

Agriculture in California was the product of the gold rush and the need to feed thousands of people starting from scratch. Hilgard reached out to the equally new California farmers and slowly taught them about the importance of maintaining the soil in good health and how that would benefit their crops. He was tireless in his efforts. Hilgard was one of the first American academic superstars.

Berlin's Kaiser-Wilhelm Society for the Advancement of Science was founded in 1911 to promote the natural sciences in Germany. A board of trustees oversaw a set of independent directors not answerable to the state or the administration. Funds came from various sources, reinforcing the concept of independence. The Kaiser Wilhelm Society's programs led to the formation of other similar scientific institutes in the succeeding decades.

Saxony-Anhalt was the ideal place for horticultural research. When the idea of such an institute in the provinces first arose, the former chairman of the Gebr. Dippe AG Quedlinburg, Ludwig Kuehle, offered Quedlinburg and the necessary land for the new building. An Institute for Horticulture Research was approved and built in Quedlinburg.

These institutions were able to build on a solid base from the nineteenth century. In order to keep the industry stable, yet moving forward at the same time, the growers banded together to create professional organizations. First came the German Gardening Association, founded in 1872, followed by the General

German Gardening League in 1890. By 1924, the National Association of German Nurseries took over. No one could doubt their high level of professionalism, and that reputation reached beyond Saxony Anhalt and Thuringia. It meant that gardening was accepted as a respectable profession on a par with other respectable work in the middle classes.

The existence of these significant groups did not preclude private industry from taking action. Dippe expanded the company's own research facilities and hired Gustav Becker to supervise the laboratories. Cooperation between the two basic science establishments proved beneficial to the company.

After the end of World War Two and the confiscation of the Dippe Company, Gustav Becker became chairman of the Institute, which the department of agricultural science had appropriated. He did not agree with the government's policies and was forced to take early retirement towards the end of the 1960s. Becker was an excellent scientist who thought in practical terms and made great contributions to horticultural research and its applications.

A second horticultural institute was built in Vienna. Hans Stubbe became its first chairman. It only existed for two years, being forced to close because of World War Two. Becker had it moved to Gatersleben near Quedlinurg. Hans Stubbe remained chairman until his death in 1989.

With reunification, these institutes were modernized at great expense and undertook new assignments and projects. The International Seed Processing GmbH arose from this source. The DDR had created this company in 1946 to trade in horticultural crops under the name of the German Seed Company (Deutsche Saatgutgesellschaft - DSG) and later on under VEB Saat- und Pflanzgut für gartenbauliche Kulturarten (a government-owned seed and plant company).

A Swiss company bought the business after the political changes of 1989, reorganized it, and sold it. ISP GmbH now produces standard seed as well as breeding new varieties for commercial horticulture. It works with ten vegetable species as well as numerous varieties of flowers and ornamental herbs bred in house.

Seed cultivation and horticultural science rose to a new level of importance in the late 1940s and were given official blessing. The former seed companies Dippe, Mette, and Schreiber were involved in a new umbrella project as VEG members. A facility was built for propagating ornamental plant and vegetable seed on a very large scale encompassing the August Bebel Seed Company, another member of the VEG.

August Bebel was required to provide space for ornamental plants. These premises were expanded in 1957 and 1958. They were called Weyhegarten. Each year more Quedlinburg lots were incorporated into the program, identified by the names "Weyhe" and "Kleersgarten." The work force voted to join the VEG in 1962 to prevent the business from closing and thus threatening their jobs. Seven years later, in 1969, the workers were then asked to choose between continuing to be part of the VEG or to become an independent business with government management. They chose to join a new VEG called Saatzucht Zierpflanzen Erfurt (Ornamental Plant Seed Growers of Erfurt) which had been in existence since 1964. The production profile remained unchanged.

The Weyhegarten was used to propagate many potted plants such as begonia, calceolaria, cyclamen, gloxinia, and primulas, and the Kleersgarten was used to grow seeds for annuals and biennials as well as perennials. After land belonging to Hesse, Franke in Rieder and Ballenstedt was incorporated into the organization in 1972, other plants, mostly foliage, roses, and freesias, were propagated. The open fields were assigned to the LPG.

There had been an earlier merger in 1964. Weyrgarten became part of Betriebsteil Quedlinburg des VEG Saatzucht Zierpflanzen Erfurt. Shortly afterwards, Wehrenpfennig, Teupel, parts of Hesse and Franke in Rieder, and Walter Dietzmann in Zoerbig were all incorporated into this state-run organization. Everyone had to produce their quota of ornamental seedlings. Flower shops were also opened in Quedlinburg, Rieder, and Ballenstedt.

W. Dietzmann in Zoerbig voluntarily joined the Quedlinburg VEG and produced pelargonium and fuchsia seedlings under glass. The glass was in a deplorable condition and required constant repairs. Due to the distance between Zoerbig and Quedlinburg, all this became difficult to coordinate.

In 1969 the Quedlinburg open-air seed growing operation added two new companies, Haake & Co and Storbeck and Dannemann (from Weddersleben) to the co-operative, which became known as the "Kooperationsgemeinschaft Quedlinburger Zuchtbetriebe" (Quedlinburg Plant Breeders Cooperative). The resulting increase in land made it easier to implement modern technology and the different growers cooperated. After the state takeover in 1972, the August Bebel VEG took charge of the cooperative in 1974. The whole Quedlinburg VEG Ornamental Plant Seed Growers of Erfurt was assigned to the August Bebel VEG in 1979.

The old facilities started to be dismantled in the 1980s and this continued until the beginning of the 1990s. None of the firms that had been brought into the cooperative exists anymore. Quedlinburg's fields became housing developments and the greenhouses were all taken down and replaced with apartment buildings and new roads.

The city's worldwide reputation in horticulture had already begun to fade after the war. Now, except for a few historic markers and street names as reminders of the past, there's hardly any more horticultural production left. The younger generations may not even know there ever was such an industry in their town.

This train of events is not unique to Quedlinburg. It happens whenever pressure from urban centers overtakes slower, old-fashioned uses of the land. As population increases, the value of land shoots up way past the return from agriculture or horticulture. If the land is then taxed at its new market value, the farmer is driven to sell or go out of business. Because of this trajectory, arable land continues to be taken out of cultivation at an alarming rate in many countries. Once paved over, the land is useless agriculturally for aeons.

In 1990 a relative of P.J. Schmidt, D. Schmidt, started the meristem and tissue culture lab "In Vitro Plant Service." While in the GPD (another state-run organization for perennials in Quedlinburg), he worked on the propagation of perennials and orchids. He very generously offered this as a service for other companies. After 1990, the GPD Perennial organization turned into a firm called "Floraque Stauden & Zierpflanzen e.G. (Floraque Perennials and Decorative Plants).

Starting in 1990 after the reunification, many of the old private companies' buildings and other property that had become part of the GDR's agricultural production collectives (VEG Saatzucht August Bebel) were turned over to the German Democratic Republic's Treuhand (Public Trust). The Swiss company, Mauser, bought land and buildings in an attempt to recreate Quedlinburg's former seed producing industry, but it ended in liquidation. As of 2013, the fate of these estates and buildings that were part of the communist horticultural collectives was still up in the air.

The big greenhouse complex of the former VEG Vockerode near Dessau is another horticultural business that has not survived the past twenty-five years. Just like many other facilities in the DDR, it was strategically placed next to power plants in order to take advantage of the nearby accumulated warmth. Vegetables and cut flowers were grown on twenty-five hectares under foil-covered greenhouses.

These actions made little professional sense, but were just imposed by the local party of the DDR and never amounted to anything. The efforts to make improvements after 1990 also ended in failure. There was a similar story with greenhouses on the outskirts of Halle and Magdeburg, or Schoenbeck.

Many growers in the 1960s and 1970s placed mixed-use greenhouses next to their livestock shelters with the hopes of creating synergy to benefit the community. It was most probably due to requirements by the state government. The desired result never came about. Two LPGs (Landwirtschaftliche Produktionsgenossenschaft, (agricultural collective) Florian Geyer in Aschersleben and LPG Wittenberg did manage to prosper for a time. LPG Wittenberg continued the tradition of growing mayflowers (*Epigae repens*) but neither exists any more.

There was one successful operation in Genthin, a small town in Saxony near the Elbe River, run by Gerhard Pauer, a friend of Klaus Hoffmann. He was a remarkable horticulturist. Using his managerial talent and business acumen, he built an enormous greenhouse and foil-covered facility. After 1990, he modernized it prudently, creating a useful template for the rest of Germany. Pauer shifted from coal to oil heating and installed automatic irrigation systems for water and fertilizer.

Even though this firm changed ownership in 2011, it continues to thrive. It was bought by a successful Dresden company that wanted to find a cost-effective method of transporting its garden products and potted plants. They now produce window box plants and other small retail items, which are sold by large general chains throughout Germany.

## Older nurseries

It is believed that there were twenty-three nurseries and garden supply businesses in Quedlinburg in 1908. This number remained more or less constant throughout the first world war. Their output was dwarfed by the forty-eight large seed growers and seedling producers. In 1914, they provided sixty percent of the world's supply of flower seeds on farmland in and around the city of Quedlinburg.

The seed growing business spread to other towns in the region. Koennern an der Saale, Aschersleben, Ballenstedt, Bernburg or Halberstadt, and even Magdeburg and numerous other places around Magdeburg (Magdeburg Boerde) became centers for seed cultivation. Firma Meisert was a very good nursery in Koennern.

Carl Heinrich Franke and Hermann Hesse (no relation to the well-known author of that name) from Gemarkung Rieder/Gernrode raised dahlia bulbs and pansy seeds. The Staudenbetrieb (Perennial Nursery) Weinreich in Wolmirstedt was very productive. Under the DDR it was a member of the

Quedlinburg cooperative, GPG. The original owner was able to get the business back in 1989, and now runs it under the name Floragarten Weinreich.

After reunification, official cooperatives could continue operating, albeit under new laws laid down in accordance with the rules of the Federal Republic of Germany as well as the content of the Unification Treaty of 1990. The decision of the members for or against this path was binding. A few made an effort to continue, but it was an untenable situation. There was no way they could survive in the new climate. Distribution of shares, sometimes shares of land, was only possible after years of work, if at all.

Many obstacles prevented the continued existence of cooperatives. Sloppy, haphazard practices meant that greenhouses, hothouses, or storehouses had been built on pieces of land belonging to many different owners. Building permits had been ignored.

It was what we would today call a conglomerate of affiliated companies, but it was nothing like market-based reality. The VEB handled 370 different types of plants, leading to 2,250 identified varieties (cultivars) that were propagated, licensed, and sent to market. The breeding and cultivation area occupied 450,000 hectares. There were fifty-seven breeding stations employing 2,500 workers for about 4,000 hectares of nursery gardens.

None of it helped.

## Conclusion

This long recital of individuals and small firms may have seemed like a slog, but these are the significant details which Klaus Hoffmann noticed and recorded. History is made of grand sweeping phenomena and local events on the ground. Both are necessary to understand what took place.

It is possible that the heyday of the Thuringian and Saxon floral industries had already passed after World War Two, to be finally eclipsed by the enormous economic forces affecting floriculture in the rest of the postwar world, but it might not have been as brutal while it played out. The cost of labor and of heating both seriously threatened Northern European horticulture in the 1970s, but imagination and flexibility were able to save great parts of it. Dutch floriculture still flourishes, even though faced with the same problems. There is also still a very vigorous German horticulture industry, but far away from the region discussed here. The great natural resources of water and climate have not been enough to permit a robust revival.

Now Erfurt and Quedlinburg are both pretty tourist attractions, with token gardens and parks, but all the old gardens, greenhouses, and fields that made these places famous for floriculture have been paved over. There are a few street names commemorating the old firms and one or two statues. This book can be considered to be an elegy for a way of life which has vanished.

# Acknowledgements

The author is indebted to the following people for invaluable help.

Rolf Bielau, Erfurt

Hans-Joachim Brinkjans, Berlin

Antonia Feindura, Dresden

Antje Kresser, Erfurt

Albrecht Meinel, Heimburg

Professor Gerhard Roebbelen, Goettingen

Joachim Schaier, Erfurt

Dr Clemens Wimmer, horticultural librarian, Berlin

Jens Wuencher, Stuttgart

Maps
The maps were prepared by Molly Roy, specialist cartographer

Editing
Christine Wenc copy edited the manuscript

# References

Baumann, Martin and Steffen Rassloff, eds, 2011 "Blumenstadt Erfurt" Erfurt, Sutton Verlag GmbH


Bluethner, Wolf-Dieter in Baumann, Martin and Steffen Rasslof eds 2011
Blumenstadt Erfurt "Die Firma N.L. Chrestensen" page 177
Erfurt Sutton Verlag


Czekalla, Eberhard in Baumann, Martin and Steffen Rasslof eds 2011
Blumenstadt Erfurt "Die Firma F. C. Heinemann" page 152
Erfurt Sutton Verlag


Elsner, Wilhelm 2005 "Lebenserinnerungen Jahrgang 1921 Gartner"
Published by the author

Fulbrook, Mary 2005. "The People's State: East German society from Hitler to Honecker"
New Haven and London Yale University Press


Groning, Gert and Joachim Wolschke-Bulmahn, eds., 1997. "Grüne Biografien"
Berlin Hannover Patzer Verlag


Hoffmann, Klaus 2015: "Der Zierplflanzenbau in Mitteldeuschtland des 19. und 20. Jahrhunderts - Bertrachtungen über 200 Jahre Produktion und Zücthtung." ("Flower nurseries in Middle Germany in the 19th and 20th centuries- more than two hundred years of flower breeding and production.")
Notschriften Verlag Radebeul


Iordachi, Constantin and Arnd Bauerkämper, eds. 2014. "The Collectivisation of Eastern Europe: comparison and entanglements"
Budapest and New York Central European University Press.


Kratzsch, Georg, "Development of the Publicly Owned System" in Roebbelen, Gerhard, ed.: 2008

Die Entwicklung der Pflanzenzuchtung in Deuschtland
(1908 – 2008)
100 Jahre GFP e.V. eine Dokumentation
Goettingen Gesellschaft fur Pflanzensuchtung


Nelson, Arvid 2005
Cold War Ecology: forests, farms and people in the East German
landscape 1945 – 1989
New Haven, Connecticut Yale University Press


Roebbelen, Gerhard 2009 "Biographisches Lexikon zur
Geschichte der Pflanzenzuchtung"
Gottingen Gesellschaft fur Pflanzenzuchtung


United States Department of Agriculture: Decennial Horticultural
Census
Washington DC


Vagt, Kristina 2013 "Politik durch die Blume:
Gartenbauausstellungen in Hamburg und Erfurt im Kalten
Kriege (1950 – 1974) "("Politics Through Flowers: flower shows
in Hamburg and Erfurt in the Cold War (1950 – 1974)""

Munich Hamburg Dolling und Galizt Verlag


Vavilov, Nikolai 1992 *Origin and Geography of Cultivated Plants* (translated by <u>Doris Löve</u>). 1992.
Cambridge Cambridge University Press


"Cover Picture"
Pelargoniums ("geraniums") growing in the PAC Elsner greenhouse in Dresden, Germany, by permission, Martin and Antonia Feindura.

# Index